# NEW DAD 2 BOOKS IN 1 PREGNANCY GUIDE FOR MEN + BABY CARE BOOK

HOW TO BE THE BEST PARTNER AND FATHER FROM CONCEPTION TO BIRTH AND BEYOND. EASY PROVEN METHODS TO RAISE A HEALTHY, HAPPY CHILD

**NEW DAD SUPPORT**

# CONTENTS

## PREGNANCY GUIDE FOR MEN

| | |
|---|---|
| Bonuses | 2 |
| Introduction | 5 |
| **1. BECOMING A DAD** | **7** |
| Preparing to Get Pregnant | 8 |
| Preparing Yourself Mentally | 9 |
| Preparing Your Relationship | 11 |
| **2. YOU'RE PREGNANT!** | **15** |
| Revealing the Pregnancy | 16 |
| The Fun Stuff | 18 |
| **3. BIRTHING AND BUILDING A BIRTH PLAN** | **25** |
| Where to Deliver | 26 |
| Methods of Birthing | 28 |
| Birth Plans | 31 |
| **4. PREPARING FOR THE WORST** | **35** |
| Miscarriages and Stillbirth | 36 |
| Ectopic Pregnancy | 37 |
| Infertility | 37 |
| Possible Pregnancy Complications | 40 |
| Screenings and Tests | 47 |
| **5. FIRST TRIMESTER** | **53** |
| Week 1 & 2 | 54 |
| Week 3 | 55 |
| Week 4 | 56 |
| Week 5 | 57 |
| Week 6 | 58 |
| Week 7 | 60 |
| Week 8 | 61 |
| Week 9 | 63 |
| Week 10 | 64 |
| Week 11 | 66 |
| Week 12 | 67 |

| | |
|---|---|
| 6. SECOND TRIMESTER | 69 |
| Week 13 | 70 |
| Week 14 | 72 |
| Week 15 | 74 |
| Week 16 | 78 |
| Week 17 | 79 |
| Week 18 | 81 |
| Week 19 | 83 |
| Week 20 | 84 |
| Week 21 | 86 |
| Week 22 | 87 |
| Week 23 | 88 |
| Week 24 | 88 |
| Week 25 | 91 |
| Week 26 | 92 |
| 7. THIRD TRIMESTER | 95 |
| Week 27 | 96 |
| Week 28 | 97 |
| Week 29 | 98 |
| Week 30 | 99 |
| Week 31 | 101 |
| Week 32 | 101 |
| Weeks 33 - 40+ | 102 |
| 8. GETTING READY FOR BIRTH | 105 |
| Essentials for Baby's Arrival | 106 |
| Hospital Go-Bag Essentials | 111 |
| Signs of Labor | 114 |
| The Birth | 116 |
| 9. THE FOURTH TRIMESTER | 119 |
| Finding Your Routine | 120 |
| Supporting Mom's Recovery | 122 |
| Going Back to Work | 124 |
| 10. NEW DAD HACKS | 127 |
| Pregnancy Hacks | 128 |
| Newborn Hacks | 128 |
| Afterword | 131 |
| References | 135 |

# NEW DAD'S FIRST YEAR

| | |
|---|---|
| Free Bonuses | 141 |
| Introduction | 145 |
| **1. BIRTH AND FIRST DAY** | **151** |
| Routine Vaginal Delivery | 152 |
| Non-Routine Vaginal Delivery | 154 |
| C-Section | 155 |
| If Your Baby Was Born Premature | 157 |
| All About Apgar Test and Scores | 158 |
| First-Time Dad Tips | 160 |
| **2. COMING HOME WITH YOUR NEW BABY** | **161** |
| Leaving the Hospital | 161 |
| Going Home | 164 |
| Your Baby's Big 3: Feeding, Crying, and Sleeping | 167 |
| **3. BABY CARE 101** | **179** |
| Swaddling | 180 |
| Changing Diapers | 181 |
| Holding Your Baby | 185 |
| Bathing Your Baby | 188 |
| Clothing Your Baby | 191 |
| Basic Healthcare | 192 |
| Finding Childcare | 195 |
| **4. YOUR BABY'S FIRST MONTH** | **197** |
| Feeding | 198 |
| Sleeping | 199 |
| Bonding With Baby | 200 |
| Learning | 201 |
| Keeping Baby Safe | 201 |
| How is Mom? | 202 |
| How is Dad? | 204 |
| **5. GETTING THE HANG OF IT** | **205** |
| Month 2 | 206 |
| Month 3 | 212 |
| **6. NEWBORN TO INFANT** | **219** |
| Month 4 | 220 |
| Month 5 | 228 |

| | |
|---|---|
| 7. HALF WAY THERE | 237 |
|     Month 6 | 238 |
|     Month 7 | 244 |
| 8. READY, SET, GO! | 255 |
|     Month 8 | 256 |
|     Month 9 | 261 |
| 9. BYE BYE BABY | 269 |
|     Month 10 | 270 |
|     Month 11 | 276 |
| 10. FIRST BIRTHDAY | 283 |
| 11. PARENTING STYLES 101 | 291 |
|     What's *Your* Parenting Style? | 291 |
|     Attachment Parenting | 292 |
|     Authoritative/Parent-Led Parenting | 293 |
|     Free-Range Parenting | 294 |
|     Green or Eco-Friendly Parenting | 296 |
| 12. TAKING CARE OF YOUR RELATIONSHIPS | 299 |
|     Self-care and Where to Find Support | 300 |
|     Finances | 301 |
|     New Dad Tips and Tricks | 302 |
|     Resources | 305 |
|     Free Bonuses | 307 |
|     Bibliography | 311 |
|     About the Author | 317 |

© **Copyright 2022 - All rights reserved.**

The content contained within this book may not be reproduced, duplicated or transmitted without direct written permission from the author or the publisher.

Under no circumstances will any blame or legal responsibility be held against the publisher, or author, for any damages, reparation, or monetary loss due to the information contained within this book, either directly or indirectly.

Legal Notice:

This book is copyright protected. It is only for personal use. You cannot amend, distribute, sell, use, quote or paraphrase any part, or the content within this book, without the consent of the author or publisher.

Disclaimer Notice:

Please note the information contained within this document is for educational and entertainment purposes only. All effort has been executed to present accurate, up to date, reliable, complete information. No warranties of any kind are declared or implied. Readers acknowledge that the author is not engaged in the rendering of legal, financial, medical or professional advice. The content within this book has been derived from various sources. Please consult a licensed professional before attempting any techniques outlined in this book.

By reading this document, the reader agrees that under no circumstances is the author responsible for any losses, direct or indirect, that are incurred as a result of the use of the information contained within this document, including, but not limited to, errors, omissions, or inaccuracies.

# PREGNANCY GUIDE FOR MEN

## HOW TO BE THE BEST SUPPORTIVE PARTNER AND FATHER, FROM CONCEPTION TO BIRTH AND BEYOND. PLUS 10 LIFE HACKS FOR NEW DADS

## Free Bonuses

### Free Bonus #1 Baby Financial Planning

In this book, you will learn all about the financial considerations of having a baby.

### Free Bonus #2 10 Activities to Learn Parenting Skills

In this book, you will get tips on how to build parenting skills even before the baby is born.

**Free Bonus #3 Authentic Connections**

In this book, you will learn new skills to help you nurture your connection with your partner and bring it to a whole new level.

To get bonuses, scan this QR code with your cell phone

# INTRODUCTION

> "Making the decision to have a child is momentous. It is to decide forever to have your heart go walking around outside your body." – Elizabeth Stone

So, it's officially time. You and your partner have decided to pursue growing your family. First, congratulations on taking the next incredible step on your journey! Becoming a parent is a monumental and life-changing step in anyone's life. Making the choice to become parents takes your relationship to the next level, and though we may know people who are parents—we may have watched all kinds of media about having a child, or read articles and books—nothing can truly prepare us for the wonder that is pregnancy, childbirth, and parenthood until we're in the thick of it.

Today, the responsibilities of each parent is shifting; more families rely on dual incomes than that of our grandparents, as well as some of our parents. The impact of pregnancy on the mind and body of those who bear children is better understood, and we can now better support our partners after they've brought our children into the world. We can better understand the pressures of parenting while working, making us better companions when our partner needs us the most.

In the following chapters, we cover the whole story of pregnancy from conception to birth and beyond. Everything from the possible complications and difficulties of conception and pregnancy, to how to be the best father and partner when the new baby is brought home.

 "A baby makes love stronger, the days shorter, the nights longer, savings smaller, and a home happier."
—Unknown

# CHAPTER 1
# BECOMING A DAD

> "Fatherhood is the greatest thing that could ever happen. You can't explain it until it happens; it's like telling somebody what water feels like before they've ever swam in it." – Michael Bublé

IN THE MONTHS leading up to conception, there is work to be done to make sure that both you and your partner have balanced and healthy expectations of one another. When we first start planning to conceive, we can sometimes think that we just have to get romantic and intimate with our partner at the right time, and that's all there is to it. In a lot of cases, it can take time for the pregnancy to come about. Don't panic if you're not immediately pregnant because you did the deed exactly 14 days after the first day of your partner's period. There's plenty that can be done to help you and your partner get ready to conceive.

## PREPARING TO GET PREGNANT

Physically, there is just as much that goes into Dad getting ready for the point of conception as there is for Mom. After all, you're looking to plant a high-quality seed here, and you want to be healthy if you're going to give yourself the best chance of conceiving. Choosing to conceive sometimes means starting months in advance so that you can hopefully have a healthy child without too much struggling to conceive. In order to give yourself the best chances of conception, the following list can help you increase your fertility:

- **Speak to your doctor.** Whether it's getting a physical or having your sperm count tested, speaking to your doctor can help you both get healthy, and possibly pinpoint any areas that may be working against you in conceiving a child with your partner. Your doctor will work with you to identify if there are any medications that you're on that may inhibit your ability to have a child, as well as look into any dietary or sleep changes that may need to be made. Depending on what you do for work, they may also advise you to stay away from certain types of chemicals, such as solvents and pesticides. Of course, adding in an exercise regimen if you don't already have one may be recommended.
- While you're there, get a better look at your medical history. Knowing if there are any serious diseases or genetic abnormalities that run in your family will help you know what to look for when you have your own child. If you know what you're up against, you can be better equipped for the possibilities regarding your child's health and well-being down the road.

- **Keep your boys cool.** If you're a briefs man, it may be time to trade them in for some boxers. The same goes for staying out of the sauna, the hot tub, or extra hot showers and baths. Heat can harm and kill the sperm cells that you're hoping to put to work, so making sure that your testicles are staying cool is a good way to help increase sperm count. There is still some debate over whether briefs are the biggest problem in terms of capturing and retaining heat, but especially if you're concerned about a low sperm count, getting some extra air flow in there can't hurt.
- **It's time to stop the party.** Alcohol, drugs, and cigarettes can all contribute to a lowered sperm count and even erectile dysfunction. If you're hoping to conceive, it's time to get rid of the intoxicants and focus on consuming healthier foods. Trade in the beer for a smoothie, and drop the smoking habit if you're hoping to boost the number of sperm you're working with.
- **Get the good food in you.** Having a balanced, nutritious diet can affect the health and motility of your swimmers. We're talking lean proteins, fruits, veggies, and good carbs and fats, as well as a multivitamin. Potential Dads want a diet rich in zinc, folic acid, and vitamins A, C, and E to increase the health of their sperm and keep them mobile when it comes time to attempt conception.
- **Keep the laptop on the desk and the phone out of your front pocket.** Electromagnetic radiation is suspected to be one of the big culprits of negatively impacting healthy semen. Moving your phone away from your groin, as well as keeping your laptop up on your desk instead of in your lap can minimize this radiation. The same is true with the extra heat that is put out by the machinery that can kill sperm counts.

## PREPARING YOURSELF MENTALLY

Some people can view the period of pregnancy as fairly hands-off for Dad; just make sure she gets her pregnancy cravings delivered when she wants them, and give her foot rubs when her feet swell, but after you've "planted the seed" your job is done. While yes, the brunt of the physical labor is on the new Mom, there are still things for you to prepare yourself for and educate yourself on. You're in on this team effort, even if the baby isn't firmly squared away in your abdomen to grow for 40 weeks.

Ultimately, your job is to support your partner through pregnancy and birth. Just by the act of having picked up this book, you're already starting one of the first things you can do; learn about what is going on in Mom's body while she is pregnant. Taking the time to learn about what she will go through while pregnant and delivering the baby can make you more compassionate, as well as better equipped with knowing how to handle anything the pregnancy and delivery hurls at you. Being aware of foods that might harm the baby, medications that can be safely used, and being ready to mentally and physically support your partner are crucial to having a safe and happy pregnancy.

If you're worried about feeling like you can't do anything to support your partner, do things like taking a massage class so you can ease any pain and discomfort that grows in her body over time. Look around the house and do things without being asked. After all, taking care of the home should be a team effort, and contrary to societal jokes about bossy women, most women really don't want to be the house manager. If you don't know how to cook—learn. If you don't usually take on laundry, floors, or other household chores—step up without your partner having to hound you or beg for your help. Especially when the baby arrives, doing all these things on top of raising the child, *and* trying to heal from a major medical event, can lead to worsening symptoms of postpartum depression and anxiety if your partner doesn't feel as though they have support. Women and mothers feeling that their partner isn't an equal contributor to the home are going to be more likely to leave. Even if she steps forward as a stay-at-home or work-from-home parent, remember that she is your partner, not your maid or slave. Raising children is no easy feat, and being a stay-at-home parent is more than just watching *Price is Right* and feeding the baby.

## PREPARING YOUR RELATIONSHIP

It's so easy for us to think that nothing will change within the relationship just because you've become parents. This doesn't take into account the changes in mentality when your priorities shift to caring for your child, as well as the stress brought on by sleepless nights, the days of crying when the baby is teething or sick, or the struggles of disorders like postpartum depression, anxiety, or psychosis that Mom might face after giving birth.

Before you consider bringing a child into your life, really evaluate the health and stability of your relationship. Are you a stable and reliable partner to the person you hope will bear your child? Is she stable and ready to take on this major challenge with you? Are you two compassionate and loving towards each other, or do you tolerate each other because it's more comfortable to be with the person you can predict?

You should also consider why you and your partner are choosing to pursue having a child. Are you worried about an oncoming breakup, and think that it'll save your relationship? Or are you genuinely hoping and looking forward to raising a child with this person? Bringing a child into an unstable relationship won't save the relationship, or keep someone from leaving the relationship, so evaluate the reasons why you really want to have a child with this person.

When you've come to your conclusion, and if you've found it to be coming from a place of love, then look at how you can support your relationship's foundations going forward. If you have routines like doing date nights or movie nights, continue doing these things that are special to the two of you. Before the baby is conceived, make sure that your foundations with your partner are as stable as they can be. If you do have some concerns about moving forward, there is no shame in pursuing couples counseling if you feel your mutual understanding of each other could benefit the relationship. The most important thing about preparing your relationship before conceiving is making sure that the necessary pathways of communication are open and actively used.

Before conceiving, expectations for the pregnancy and after the baby's arrival should be spoken about and agreed upon. Get on the same page about changes in the routine, changes in scheduling, maternity and paternity leave, potential sitters, and other childcare and work schedules. These aren't things that you're going to want to fight about when you're in the thick of it. Even making sure that you're on the same page and a united front when it comes to things like discipline, religion, and schooling can go a long way in preventing major disagreements that could have been avoided. Take the time, and really paint out your vision for the future, and listen to your partner's vision of the future. It's perfectly normal for those visions to not perfectly align, but be prepared to compromise now, instead of later when you might learn just how different your views are compared to your partner.

**Take some time to answer the questions below together.**

1. Why do we want to start a family?

2. Is now the best time?

3. How much will it cost? Can we afford it?

4. Will we both continue to work after the birth? If so, what will we do for childcare?

5. How do we want to parent? How will we discipline?

6. What values or religious beliefs do we want to pass on?

7. How will we address issues in getting pregnant?

8. What does the future of our family look like? How many kids do we want? And how soon?

# CHAPTER 2
# YOU'RE PREGNANT!

> "Fathering is not something perfect men do, but something that perfects the man." – Frank Pittman

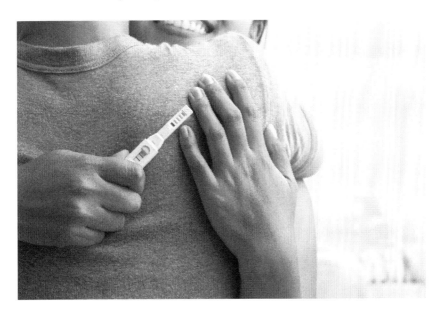

IT HAPPENED—YOU got through the obstacles, and now you've got that positive pregnancy test sitting on your counter. Before we get into the nitty-gritty of what's going on inside of Mom's uterus and how you can best help her, let's take a look at the fun stuff you get to do now that you're officially expecting.

## REVEALING THE PREGNANCY

Pregnancy announcements vary per couple. Some people may wait until they're past the 12-week mark to negate the riskiest time period for miscarriage; others may be rushing out to tell everyone right away. There isn't a wrong way to go about announcing your pregnancy. When considering announcing the pregnancy, think about the following points so that you can best choose how and when to announce your newest arrival:

- Consider your timeline. If your partner has experienced a miscarriage before, give yourselves time to get past the riskiest period of time before announcing the pregnancy. At least this way, you can negate the painful reminders if a miscarriage does happen. Truly, there's no worse feeling after having just miscarried than seeing an acquaintance that asks about the pregnancy, just to be reminded of your loss and having to talk about it. If you want to be careful, take the time.
- Consider *who* you're telling. While we may be excited to tell everyone under the sun about the baby on the way, we also want to be able to break the news ourselves. Before you break out the big announcement, make sure that the people that you're telling early are people that you trust—that aren't going to run their mouths and ruin the excitement of the announcement for you and your partner. If you know that someone on either side of the family is way too excited about becoming a grandparent, aunt, or uncle, consider waiting to tell them about the pregnancy until you're just about to announce it, so that they can't excitedly take the wind out of your sails.
- Who needs to be told before the main announcement? In the case of certain jobs that may be harmful to a pregnancy, Mom

may need to tell her employer about the pregnancy sooner than later. This is particularly important if the job comes with a lot of heavy lifting, physical exertion, or working with potentially harmful chemicals.
- Aside from an employer, we all have a list of people who we know would be hurt if they weren't personally told about the pregnancy before the rest of the world finds out on social media, so talk to your partner about letting these people in on the secret and when.
- Plan the announcement itself. Nobody says that you have to have a major grand reveal, or that you have to go all the way out. Do what feels the most comfortable for both you and your partner, and what you feel is most representative of you as a couple and family. Some people use their pets as a way to introduce the pregnancy to the world, others like to do a photo set that goes up on social media. There are hundreds upon hundreds of ideas online if you're looking for inspiration.

## THE FUN STUFF

The "fun stuff" is usually the keepsake items and family events that revolve around the pregnancy. These are events that you'll look back on and show your child. You'll want to record these special moments, where you can truly celebrate with those that matter the most to you. Some of these occasions will also be a chance to get a little bit of help from family and friends. This is so important when it comes to getting everything you need to help you care for your baby.

*Weekly Progress Photos*

You and your partner can really start this at any time. Some like to wait to start seeing the baby bump forming, and some like to take pictures right from the beginning so they can best see exactly when the baby bump started to form, and the changes that their body went through from start to finish. These progress photos are often cherished, and can make a fantastic collage, culminating with a picture of you holding the little one after you've gotten out of the hospital with Mom and baby.

*Pregnancy Journal*

Pregnancy journals are both a helpful resource and a lovely keepsake. This is where Mom can track all of the happenings in her pregnancy: different cravings, the variety of symptoms, the first kicks, absolutely anything she wants. Depending on her intent, it can become a keepsake item that is passed down to the child, or something that she keeps for herself. Bringing it to appointments with you can also help, so she can reference notes if there was a concerning symptom, to add in any sonogram pictures that are printed off, or to be able to easily reference questions she might have for the doctor, or any ideas that she might need confirmation on from her medical professional.

*Bump Casting*

Bump casting is using some form of plaster or otherwise skin-safe molding material to get a cast of the baby belly shortly before Mom gives birth. These can be turned into lovely art pieces to be decorated later with the baby's handprints, or made into a decorative sculpture to commemorate the pregnancy.

## Baby Names

Choosing a baby name is just as fun as it can be intimidating. Are you going to choose a family name, or is the child going to get their own unique name? When choosing a baby name, there is one simple rule: it takes both parents saying "yes" for a name to be an option, but one "no" to take it off the table. If someone says no, the name needs to be dropped, and continue the search for a new name. If you're choosing not to find out the gender of the baby, it can help to have three name options: one feminine, one masculine, and one gender neutral. Some parents find that it helps to see the baby before choosing a name, so do what fits best for you.

Some people also choose to withhold the name until the baby arrives. This can be for a variety of reasons; some simply find it fun, and will refer to the baby as "Baby A" or something along those lines so that they can introduce the baby to the world with their real name. In other situations, if you know someone within the family is going to push for a family name that the two of you don't agree on—or especially if either of you have that one family member who insists that you name the baby after them for whatever reason—keeping the name secret keeps people from pushing opinions on the name that you're choosing for your child. It can also keep other people from attempting to ruin the name for you, depending on what your relationship is with your family.

## Baby Showers/Diaper Parties

Depending on where you're from and any family traditions, some people may choose to throw their own baby shower, while others have family or friends throw the party on their behalf. There are a few variations on the traditional baby shower in more recent years. Traditionally, a baby shower is more for the women of the family and friend circle, and is primarily centered around Mom and baby. However, many have started to do them "Jack and Jill" style, centering around Mom and Dad. The baby shower is where you usually get lots of the baby essentials: clothes, toys, books, blankets—and depending on the financial situation of those participating, sometimes even strollers, high chairs, or whichever other gifts you may have listed on the baby registry to let people know what you need and what you'd like to have for the baby. Guests play games centered around the baby, like guessing how big the baby belly is, sometimes holding raffles regarding the baby's weight or when they'll make their appearance. Every area tends to hold their own baby shower traditions, but food, games, and lots of talk about the baby are typical for baby showers.

Diaper parties are often centered around Dad. While there are still some of the usual baby shower games present, diaper parties tend to be a little less "all about baby." Traditionally, the guests of the diaper party will bring one or two boxes of diapers each, enjoy a barbecue, and otherwise enjoy their own games. There may be betting on the baby's arrival, or other games involving the baby's weight or length when they are born, but just like the baby shower, the games and traditions tend to be reliant on the area that you are from.

*Gender Reveals*

Gender reveals can be fun… if done safely. The inventor of the gender reveal party, Jenna Karvunidis, has expressed her own horror and regret about the dangerous extremes that gender reveal parties have become. If you choose to have a gender reveal party, don't resort to explosives; as we've seen in the past, while we may enjoy having a dramatic announcement, do so with less fire and explosives that can result in wildfires and casualties. If you choose to have a gender reveal party with your loved ones, try popping balloons or cutting cakes with the color associated with your baby's gender hidden inside.

*Baby Registry*

The baby registry is a great way to let others help you, as well as a way to keep track of what you may still need to get. Parents tend to be hesitant of putting expensive items onto their registry, but don't fear the expensive items! Sometimes there are multiple people who want to pool funds to buy something larger, or someone may have the resources to buy the one you like. Other times, knowing that you still need something like a stroller may mean that other parents looking at your registry might already have the item in good shape to give to you. If the people looking to buy a gift for your child don't have the resources for the expensive items, letting them know what kinds of blankets, toys, and other supplies you may need lets them find something within their budget, and takes some pressure off of you and your partner. List anything you can think of, and refer to the registry regularly so that you know what you still need to get. Of course, this also helps your friends and family know what to get, instead of defaulting to a tiny onesie or another teddy bear.

*Maternity Photos*

These are the special mementos before and after the due date, where you can really capture the beauty of the pregnancy. Some people like to do this a few times over the course of the pregnancy, while some couples really like to wait until the bump is about as big as it's going to get. Doing a maternity shoot is a great way for an exhausted mother to feel beautiful, and for both Mom and Dad to really gain an appreciation for what her body is doing. Some maternity shoots are entirely focused on the mother, but lots of people also incorporate the father as well. After all, you certainly helped kickstart the pregnancy to begin with.

List 3 or more ideas of fun ways to announce the pregnancy.

## PREGNANCY CHECKLIST

### FIRST TRIMESTER

| | |
|---|---|
| Calculate your baby's due date | Figure out your finances |
| Talk to your insurance company | Follow a healthy lifestyle |
| Choose a doctor/midwife | Take your prenatal vitamins |
| Schedule your first prenatal visits and tests | Make a dentist appointment |
| Thing plan your maternity leave | Start taking belly photos |

### SECOND TRIMESTER

| | |
|---|---|
| Make appointment for second-trimester tests | Find a prenatal exercise class |
| Keep track of blood pressure | Shop for maternity clothes |
| Find out baby's gender at ultrasound | Sign up for a childbirth class |
| Get multiple marker screening test | Track your weight gain |
| Know the symptoms and risks of preeclampsia | Research baby names |

### THIRD TRIMESTER

| | |
|---|---|
| Doctor exams | Learn about the stages of labor |
| Blood test for anemia and antibodies | Prepare for breastfeeding |
| Test for group B strep | Prepare house for baby |
| Glucose tolerance test | Make food for After baby's born |
| Get the Tdap vaccine | Pack hospital bag |

# CHAPTER 3
# BIRTHING AND BUILDING A BIRTH PLAN

 "A baby fills a place in your heart that you never knew was empty." — Unknown

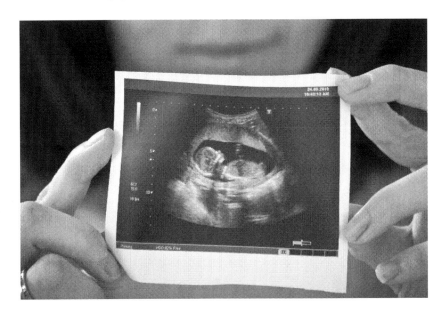

AT SOME POINT, you and your partner are going to have to discuss the ideal birthing scenario. The most common method of

thinking is that the only way to give birth is to show up at the hospital, and either push the baby out vaginally, or have the baby surgically birthed by cesarean section. This isn't the case, and there are a variety of ways to give birth that will allow for a safe and comfortable delivery, depending on the desires of you and your partner. Mom needs to feel secure and comfortable when giving birth, so listen closely to her needs and desires regarding the birth.

## WHERE TO DELIVER

### *The Hospital*

The hospital is one of the most common places that women will plan to give birth. Birth is, though very natural, a major medical procedure. The body goes through incredible changes, and for some, it can be traumatic if something goes wrong. For many, the hospital is the preferred place to be for delivery so that, should anything go wrong, they are already in a medical center that is immediately prepared to intervene in any emergency scenario.

Within the hospital, you will have medical doctors (MDs) and in some, registered midwives who will supervise and assist in the birth. Typically, the hospital is equipped with special rooms for labor and maternity. These will come with varying levels of comfort; some are equipped with large comfortable chairs, while others have birthing tubs and other amenities to provide comfort and the ideal birthing scenario for mothers. Before choosing the hospital that will become the place your child is born, arrange for a tour, and consider things like the distance from home, how long it will take to get there from locations like your home or work, and the kinds of amenities that will be available to your partner as she brings your child into the world.

The downside when considering a hospital birth is that there is a significantly higher chance of unwanted medical intervention if the birth isn't moving along to the doctor's liking. While the doctor absolutely does have your health and safety in mind, you have to consider that they're busy within the hospital, and work long hours—

this could mean that they might rush the labor, and try to move quickly onto the next patient, or get out after an already long day. If they can see that artificial hormones will make labor go faster, they may decide to use them, rather than just allowing the body to perform as it needs to. It's best to have a conversation with your doctor at a regularly scheduled visit well ahead of the birth.

*Home*

Home births are another option, especially for those who are uncomfortable with hospital births. If you and your partner choose a home birth, consider finding a registered midwife who will be able to supervise and assist in the birth. Registered midwives come with a whole host of medical knowledge should they need to intervene, but they are also trained to assist in allowing the body to do what it needs to, without rushing the job.

On the positive side, home births mean that any number of people can be invited to the birth if the mother wants more than one or two people for support (which is the typical limit that hospitals have for labor and delivery rooms). Her comfort items are already there, and she can labor where she feels most at ease. This also negates transport to and from the hospital, and means that her preferred foods and clothing are already in reach.

The downside is that if there were to be anything wrong that is outside of the care a midwife can provide, you'll likely have to rush to a hospital. Home births aren't recommended unless you've had a low-risk pregnancy overall.

*Birthing Centers*

Birthing centers often provide the best of hospital and home deliveries to the mother—the setting is far more comfortable than a hospital, and is specialized to labor and delivery, and if there aren't medical professionals on hand ready to intervene if necessary, the birthing center is typically quite close to local hospitals. There is no shortage of support for laboring women in a birthing center, in the form of midwives and doulas alike. (Doulas are not medical professionals, but are trained to assist a laboring and birthing mother through the process.) A birthing center can provide assistance in any way except for a c-section, which is the principal reason a mother might be transferred from the birthing center to the local hospital. If the pregnancy is high risk, a birthing center isn't recommended.

## METHODS OF BIRTHING

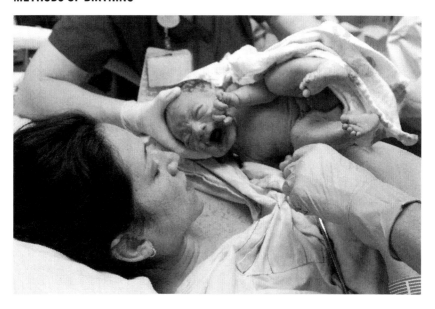

When the time comes to push, Mom might not have the utmost control over the exact method of birth she uses. This is going to depend heavily on the circumstances and the health of her pregnancy. As long as she is having a healthy pregnancy and the birth moves according to plan, she should be able to have the birth the way she desires.

*Unassisted Vaginal Delivery*

The unassisted vaginal delivery is the "all natural" approach. This means that Mom isn't using any kind of medication, whether it's for pain relief or to make labor move along more quickly. While a doctor, midwife, or doula may be present, the goal is for these professionals to not intervene, but to simply be there for support, and of course, to catch the baby as it enters the world. This type of birth can be held in the hospital, in a birthing center, or in the home.

**The Bradley Method** is often the preferred method taught and used by midwives. The course for the Bradley Method takes place over 12 weeks, teaching breathing, pain management, and nutrition that go along with caring for yourself and your partner through the end of the pregnancy. They also teach what to expect when the baby arrives, and how to best care for yourselves as you care for your little bundle of joy.

**Water births** are one method of unassisted childbirth that can help to make Mom more comfortable as she labors and pushes. Many birthing centers and some hospitals have tubs that are available for use, and a small pool or tub can be arranged in the home for home births. The warm water helps to soothe the mother through her contractions, and also allows for you to get into the tub with her to assist with the birth. A good-sized tub or pool helps the mother to get into more comfortable and natural positions to labor and deliver as comfortably as she can.

**Lamaze** can be used in both assisted and unassisted deliveries as a way to calm the body using calming, regulated breathing. The Lamaze method teaches breathing strategies, self-comfort, and soothing techniques to get you through the pain of labor. Lamaze is taught in a series of classes, teaching both Mom and her partner how to work together in getting through the birthing process as smoothly as possible, as well as teaching both partners what to be looking for and expecting when labor does begin. Typically, you should be starting Lamaze classes in the second trimester, as it does take time to learn and master the skills taught.

*Assisted Delivery*

Sometimes, the baby needs a little bit of help making their entrance into the world. If that is the case, the following methods may be what your medical professional recommends to help the process along so that you're holding your baby sooner than later, or they may utilize the method to help a baby that's in distress if labor doesn't progress as it should.

**Amniotomy** is a procedure that helps with "breaking the water" to encourage the hormone production that kickstarts labor. This may happen if the due date is long overdue, or if you're at a point in your pregnancy where a doctor is looking to help encourage labor to begin. The procedure involves using a small plastic hook to puncture a hole in the amniotic sac, releasing the fluids to encourage labor hormones to begin.

**Cesarean Section** starts by numbing the lower body through the use of an epidural administration of pain relief medications. The needle is inserted so that the medication can be administered around the spinal cord. After the medication has been administered, the mother may feel some pressure, but no pain from labor or the surgery.

During a c-section procedure, a horizontal incision is made just above the pelvic bone so that the surgeon can access the uterus. The baby (or babies) is then removed through this incision. Following the removal of the baby, the placenta is removed and the uterus cleared before stitching the incisions closed. Some surgeons may use staples on the external incision.

A c-section may be used or recommended for several reasons. If there is an emergency—such as the baby being in distress, the umbilical cord exiting before the baby does, or labor isn't progressing—the doctor may move forward with the c-section. A doctor may recommend a c-section in scenarios where the pregnancy involves multiple babies, the baby is in the breech position (meaning the head is upwards rather than downwards towards the birth canal, and repositioning was unsuccessful), or the baby is too large to pass through the pelvic canal. Placental abruption, where the placenta has separated from the uterine wall, and placenta previa, where the placenta is covering the opening to the cervix, may also be reasons why a doctor will call for a c-section to be performed. In the past, a c-section was also recommended to mothers who had previously had c-sections, but this isn't always necessary or mandated anymore.

**Episiotomy** incisions happen if the baby is stuck, or if there is any need to widen the canal so that the baby can more easily be born, especially if they are worried about the baby being under duress. The episiotomy is an incision placed along the perineum, or the tissue between the vaginal entrance and the anus, the incision often directed away from the anus. An episiotomy may heal more easily than a tear, since there will be a straight line incision.

**Forceps** are one method occasionally used by doctors to help guide the baby from the birth canal. The forceps look similar to two large spoons that are used to grasp onto the baby's head and help to guide the baby through the birth canal.

**Induced labor** is the doctor's way of manually starting labor with the use of artificial hormones to help the labor to begin. This is typically used if there is any concern for the mother or baby's wellbeing.

**Vacuum extraction** uses a small, soft cup attached to the top of the baby's head to help pull the baby free. The suction is just strong enough to grasp onto the baby's head, helping the medical professional assisting in the birth to pull the baby free from the birth canal.

*Vaginal Birth After Cesarean (VBAC)*

If this isn't your partner's first child, there is the possibility that they may have had a cesarean before. Depending on how the previous cesarean was performed, she may still be a candidate for a VBAC. As long as the previous c-section incision was done horizontally and the baby is able to fit through the pelvis, there is a likely chance that vaginal birth is an option.

## BIRTH PLANS

Your birth plan is something that may grow and develop throughout the pregnancy. This is going to be the written proposal for what should happen in the labor and delivery room. Before we get into the specifics of the birth plan, it's important to note that the birth plan should be viewed as a guide for the preferred method of birth. It can be subject to change at any moment depending on the health of the baby or the mother, especially if there are extreme circumstances. Saying "no c-section" in the birth plan won't change the need for medical intervention if there is an issue during the vaginal delivery, or if there is some form of emergency that happens before the due date. Just like some moms may say they don't want any medications for pain relief during labor, if the new Mom looks at you during labor and tells you to get her the pain meds, you get her the pain meds. Birth plans are not the be all, end all. There's no way to know how labor and delivery will go, regardless if this is your first or fifth child. The most important information to have immediately visible are things like illnesses, allergies, or anything that is absolutely crucial to know.

### *What to Include in the Birth Plan*

Think of the birth plan as the cliff notes to the ideal delivery. It shouldn't be more than a sheet, and it should hold all the crucial details related to the birth of your child. Try to keep it brief; for as much as we may want to include every single possible detail that we can think of in the "just in case" scenarios, the birth plan needs to be quickly accessible and easily scanned by a nurse, doctor, doula, or midwife that may be overseeing the birth.

- Include the basics. This should include the mother's name, your name, and the names of any other birth supports, like a doula, or any other person who should be notified that labor has begun. You should include contact information, medical information of the mother, the name and contact information of the professional who has been overseeing the pregnancy, and the name of the location where the birth is planned to take place.
- Relevant medical information. This is where you'll list any conditions the mother may have, any allergies, medications that she may be on, and any conditions that the baby may have according to tests done.
- List the birthing preferences. This pertains to the atmosphere of her labor. Does she want to be able to move about freely, be

on all fours when birthing, or have an exercise ball while laboring? Does she prefer access to a tub for water birth? A quick list of preferences can help the people supervising the birth to better accommodate her preferences so that the birth can go as smoothly and trauma-free as possible.

- Intervention preferences. At what point is Mom willing to be induced with artificial hormones? Is she okay with using forceps, or does she prefer the vacuum? At what point is she willing to accept pain medication, and in what form? Does she prefer an episiotomy, or will she only allow natural tearing to happen? This section should briefly give the people overseeing the birth the information to know—aside from an emergency scenario—when the mother is willing to have them intervene, and to what degree.
- Ideal delivery. This can include the position Mom would prefer to be in, as well as preferences regarding the need for an emergency cesarean. Who should be in the room with her? How would she like the after birth details altered if she does need an emergency surgery?
- After birth details. This is where it should be listed who is preferred to be cutting the cord, what method of feeding was chosen by the parents, and the ideal handling of the newborn upon delivery. This can mean being immediately placed on Mom's chest, or put on her belly to be allowed to crawl naturally to her breast. Some parents may prefer the baby have a moment to be wiped off and checked over before being passed to Mom or Dad, and have their own preferences regarding skin-to-skin contact. Newborn procedures such as antibiotic eye drops and the vitamin K shot should also be listed. Would you like them done right away, after the family has a moment to rest, or would you prefer to opt out?
- If Mom plans to breastfeed, she should also make note if she'd like a lactation consultant there right away. Despite the fact that breastfeeding is the most natural thing for feeding infants, it isn't all that easy for many moms, and a lactation consultant can be of enormous benefit. If she isn't planning to breastfeed,

she should make note of the types of help she will require, in terms of helping to ease the pain and production of breastmilk. You may also choose to list if you'd like a pacifier presented to the child right away.

---

Take Action

Create your birth plan:

# CHAPTER 4
# PREPARING FOR THE WORST

> "Hoping for the best, prepared for the worst, and unsurprised by anything in between."
>
> — Maya Angelou

IF YOU'RE anything like me, you like to prepare for the worst, but hope for the best. While we typically anticipate a healthy pregnancy—especially if your partner is a healthy person—it can be very difficult for us to envision that these things can happen.

## MISCARRIAGES AND STILLBIRTH

A miscarriage is often traumatic and devastating to the parents who have lost a child that they were looking forward to. Miscarriage is categorized as a sudden or spontaneous loss of the pregnancy, happening before the twentieth week of pregnancy. It's a natural response, especially for the mother, to feel that the miscarriage was their 'fault.' A miscarriage can sometimes be triggered by an accident or trauma, but otherwise, it's typically caused through the embryo or fetus not developing the way it should, and the body recognizing that this would-be infant won't be viable or survive the pregnancy. Putting blame on yourself or your partner isn't a healthy way to grieve, and it isn't an accurate train of thought to follow.

The symptoms of a miscarriage are pretty difficult to miss, especially in the later weeks of the first trimester and early second trimester. There may be spotting and bleeding to start, followed by severe cramping. After the cramping, there will be fluid and potentially fetal tissue that passes through the vaginal canal. If you manage to collect any of the fetal tissue, put it into a clean container to be brought to your local hospital or health care provider, so it can be analyzed for exactly why the miscarriage happened. This might give you insight on not only why it happened, but how to prevent a future miscarriage to the best of your ability.

Stillbirth is characterized by a loss of pregnancy after the twentieth week of pregnancy. While there are many cases of stillbirth that medical professionals cannot find a reason for, sometimes it comes down to the fetus not fully developing areas that they need to survive. It may be based on infection, chronic health conditions found within the mother, genetic and chromosomal abnormalities, or placental irregularities or problems.

If you and your partner do go through a miscarriage or stillbirth, please seek therapy from a professional to help you grieve the loss in a healthy manner.

## ECTOPIC PREGNANCY

In a standard, healthy pregnancy, once the egg is fertilized it will latch onto the lining of the uterus. This will give the embryo plenty of room to grow and develop into a healthy fetus. In the case of an ectopic pregnancy, the egg instead takes up residence in other cavities of the uterus, most often in the fallopian tube. Unfortunately, an ectopic pregnancy is not viable, and the fertilized egg cannot be manually moved to where it needs to be. Due to the danger that an ectopic pregnancy can present, an ectopic pregnancy must be terminated.

It is incredibly difficult to know that the pregnancy is ectopic without the use of an ultrasound; the pregnancy tests will come up normal, and while the pregnancy is still new, the developing embryo will have room to grow for a short period of time. Light bleeding can be one symptom, as well as shoulder pain and the need to have frequent bowel movements. This is dependent on where the blood is coming from, and which nerves are being affected by the ectopic pregnancy. If there are symptoms like severe abdominal pain, fainting, or shock, get your partner to a doctor immediately. A ruptured fallopian tube can lead to death, and needs to be treated as soon as possible.

There is no way to really prevent an ectopic pregnancy. Some things may help, like limiting the number of sexual partners, to decrease the risk of infection and pelvic inflammation. Quitting smoking can also reduce this risk, but apart from this, there's no way to anticipate or prevent the fertilized egg getting stuck somewhere it shouldn't be.

## INFERTILITY

Infertility is categorized by the inability to get pregnant after 12 months of consecutive unprotected sex. The source of the infertility can come from either partner for a vast range of reasons. There may be hormonal imbalances, issues based on drug, alcohol, or nicotine consumption, or other health problems that could potentially be resolved through medical intervention and lifestyle changes. In some cases, it may also be based on a genetic disorder, sometimes making it impossible or nearly impossible to get pregnant, especially without medical intervention. If you and your partner have been trying for longer than a year to get pregnant without success, it is recommended that you are both seen by a fertility specialist, often recommended through your primary healthcare physician.

If you are being troubled by infertility, and none of the treatments and lifestyle changes recommended by your doctor or specialist are working, the following treatments may be considered as the next step.

*Intrauterine Insemination (IUI)*

Also called artificial insemination, this process is sometimes known as the "Turkey Baster Method." The woman may be put onto medications or treatments to encourage her body to ovulate, followed by the manual depositing of the semen collected, to encourage a pregnancy to happen. This is often the process used when the issue is a low sperm count, or the motility of the sperm is quite low. Especially if the couple cannot find an explanation for exactly why they've been struggling to conceive, intrauterine insemination is often suggested as the first course of action if "doing it the old-fashioned way" isn't working for you.

## *In Vitro Fertilization (IVF)*

In vitro fertilization is the process of creating an embryo outside of the body in a lab setting. This involves the extraction of mature egg cells from the ovary via a needle, and fertilizing the egg with the sperm provided by the father-to-be. Once there is a viable embryo produced, it is then implanted into the uterus to hopefully become a successful pregnancy. IVF is a very expensive procedure; there are a variety of drugs and hormones that need to be used over a period of weeks or even months in hopes to achieve a viable, successful pregnancy.

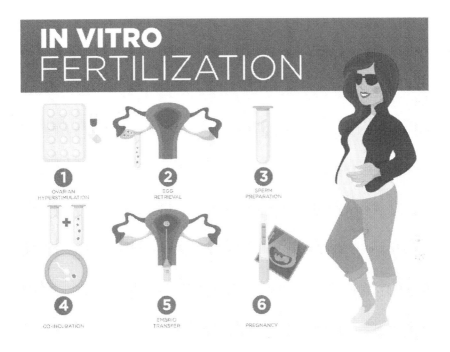

*Surrogacy*

If the issue that is causing the infertility is a 'hostile' environment within the uterus, or other issues that prevent your partner from successfully carrying an embryo or fetus to term, surrogacy is another option available to couples attempting to expand their family. In many cases, the couple may essentially go through the IVF process, but instead of the embryo being implanted into the uterus of the provider of the egg cell, the embryo is implanted into another healthy uterus for the baby to be carried to term.

## POSSIBLE PREGNANCY COMPLICATIONS

While we all hope for a healthy, uncomplicated pregnancy, there are several different disorders that may develop during pregnancy. Contrary to popular belief, pregnancy can be very hard on the human body, so it is crucial to know what you're up against should your partner develop any of these medical disorders or problems.

*Anxiety and Depression*

Not only is pregnancy a time of swift hormonal changes, it's also one of the biggest changes a person or family can make in their lives. When you combine these things, depression and anxiety can easily begin during pregnancy. If anxiety or depression do begin, it is encouraged that Mom starts visiting a therapist or psychiatrist. There are some medications that can combat the symptoms of depression and anxiety during pregnancy that are safe to use while pregnant, but some pregnant mothers largely benefit from having a therapist to do talk therapy with, in place of medications. If the symptoms of anxiety or depression do occur, it should be mentioned at the next prenatal checkup with your physician. They can recommend a doctor that suits your needs and who specializes in treating pregnant women.

*Breech Birth*

In the earlier stages of pregnancy, the baby can be facing any which way they feel like, simply due to the fact that there is so much room for them to easily move about. As the pregnancy draws to a close, the baby should get into its birthing position, with their head downwards. When a baby is in a breech position, it means that their head is up towards Mom's rib cage. This can present all kinds of challenges and dangers when it comes time to proceed with the birth. If the baby isn't successfully turned around by the time the baby is due, the medical professional supervising the pregnancy may recommend that a c-section is done to minimize the risk of injury or mortality.

*Fetal Problems*

We can never predict how a fetus will develop, and if there will be issues with organ development. While some issues may be resolved with intrauterine surgeries, others may cause the child to not be viable, or to require surgery after being born. Any fetal issues in development will be discussed with you at length by your doctor. They will go over the details of the condition, cover any options, and what to expect. For the vast array of fetal problems that can possibly arise, they really aren't as frequent as the medical dramas may lead you to believe.

*Gestational Diabetes*

Gestational diabetes occurs when a woman who previously did not have diabetes develops the condition during her pregnancy. This is often brought on due to the fluctuation and changes in her hormones affecting the production of insulin hormones from the pancreas. Developing gestational diabetes can mean that the risk of cesarean section birth is higher—due to the fetus growing too large to be birthed vaginally—as well as the possibility of developing preeclampsia. Gestational diabetes can be managed through alterations in diet and exercise, as well as medical intervention to help the body with the insulin that the body is failing to produce properly.

*High Blood Pressure*

Women who experience their blood pressure suddenly spiking higher during pregnancy develop a condition called gestational hypertension. When pregnant, women increase their blood volume, and if combined with narrowing arteries, blood carrying the oxygen and nutrients that the baby needs may have a difficult time reaching the placenta. If the baby is deprived of oxygen, growth can slow down significantly. Some women need to begin using medication to control blood pressure, and if they've developed gestational hypertension, they will be very closely monitored for the symptoms of preeclampsia, which we'll look at in more detail soon. Typically, a woman will develop gestational hypertension after the 20-week mark in her pregnancy, but it will typically resolve itself after the baby's delivery.

## Hyperemesis Gravidarum

While morning sickness might last for a few weeks for some, hyperemesis gravidarum is the persisting of morning sickness into the second, and sometimes even the third trimester. There isn't a known reason for this condition, but those who are affected by the disorder may need to go into the hospital for an IV of fluids and nutrients to replace what they aren't getting because of the inability to keep down food and fluids.

## Infections

Infections include, but aren't limited to, sexually-transmitted infections which can endanger both Mom and baby. At varying points of the pregnancy, she may be tested to make sure that she is clear from sexually transmitted disease, as well as making sure there are no bacterial infections that could be transmitted to the baby, and potentially harm them both. Any changes in discharge consistency, color, or pain in the region should be immediately checked on by a medical professional to rule out infection, and treat the infection if there is one present.

## Iron Deficiency Anemia

While pregnant, a woman's blood volume increases significantly. This can sometimes lead to iron deficiency anemia, where iron—needed for the red blood cells to carry oxygen where it needs to go—is lacking. This can result in regularly feeling fatigued and weak, sometimes even looking pale, struggling with shortness of breath, and feeling faint. Iron supplements can help with this, but if they don't appear to be working or keeping up with the job, it's best to visit your doctor for other tests to be done.

## Placenta Previa

Placenta previa is a condition characterized by the placenta covering part or all of the cervical opening. During the second and third trimesters, placenta previa may cause some bleeding, which may lead to the professional supervising the pregnancy suggesting bed rest through the end of the pregnancy to minimize the risk of harm to Mom and baby. If the bleeding is too heavy, there may be a need for Mom to be hospitalized for the remainder of the pregnancy. If there are problems with the placenta, a doctor will often recommend that a c-section should be done in order to best care for the health of Mom and baby.

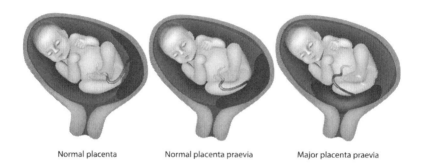

Normal placenta    Normal placenta praevia    Major placenta praevia

## Placental Abruption

During a typical healthy pregnancy, the placenta is connected to the uterine lining so that the baby can get the necessary oxygen and nutrients to thrive and develop as it should. A placental abruption means that the placenta has actually separated itself from the inner lining, depriving the baby of what it needs. Abruption can come in varying levels of severity, and can cause tenderness through the abdomen and uterus, cramping, and bleeding. While minor and moderate abruption might require bed rest and supervision, severe enough placental abruption can result in the baby needing to be delivered earlier than anticipated.

## Preeclampsia

The cause for preeclampsia isn't well understood by the medical community, but the disorder itself is the onset of high blood pressure after the second half of pregnancy. There are a number of risk factors that may lead to preeclampsia, such as pre-existing conditions like lupus, pre-existing high blood pressure, kidney disease, and diabetes. If this isn't her first pregnancy and she had preeclampsia in a previous pregnancy, Mom may be considered at risk of preeclampsia for this pregnancy. She may also be classified as high risk for preeclampsia if she is above the age of 35, considered obese, or is currently carrying multiple babies.

Preeclampsia is characterized by swelling in the face and extremities, high blood pressure, dizziness, headaches, and blurry vision. In extreme cases, it can lead to seizures, when it is then categorized as eclampsia. If Mom is diagnosed with preeclampsia or eclampsia, the only known way to cure the condition is to deliver the baby. This may require a preterm delivery, and if this is the case, the doctor will weigh the risks and benefits in her individual case. The decision will be based on the risks of maintaining the pregnancy in terms of the health of both mother and baby, weighed against the risks to the baby and mother of a preterm birth.

## Preterm Labor

If Mom goes into labor before she reaches 37 weeks of pregnancy, it is considered preterm labor. If there are already health risks involved in the pregnancy, a doctor may sometimes recommend a preterm delivery if they believe the child to be viable and the pregnancy has become too high risk. Lung and brain development isn't complete until the final weeks, so an NICU stay may be necessary for preterm deliveries.

Preterm labor may be brought on by infections, traumatic injury, shortened cervix, or previous preterm labor instances. There are a couple ways that preterm labor can be slowed or stopped: namely, cervical cerclage, which is a surgical manner of closing the cervix to keep the baby in place, or the administration of progesterone to slow and stop labor.

*Urinary Tract Infection*

During pregnancy, the risk of urinary tract infections is increased due to hormone changes and the bacteria that can thrive in this environment. The infection can affect the urethra, bladder, and even kidneys, and should be treated quickly. If UTIs continue to be a common occurrence, there may be a need for medical intervention to treat the infection regularly. If a urinary tract infection goes too long without treatment, it can result in preterm labor or a low birth weight.

## SCREENINGS AND TESTS

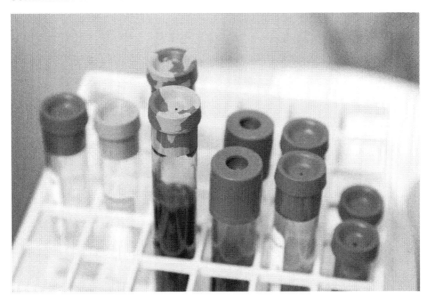

Throughout the pregnancy, there will be a variety of screenings and tests that Mom will go through. Some will be routine, whereas others will be optional screenings that you can choose with your partner whether they're necessary.

*First Trimester*

- **Blood Workups** - This will test for a variety of things: the pregnancy hormone hCG, any blood-borne sexually transmitted diseases, blood type and Rh factor, immunity to various diseases, and potential vitamin D deficiency. Depending on the result of this blood test, your healthcare provider may recommend other screening.
- **Chorionic Villus Sampling (CVS)** - In the case that you have a family history of genetic disorders, are over the age of 35, or if other tests have come back inconclusive, you may be recommended for CVS. This involves taking a small sample of the chorionic villi that protrude from the placenta. These resemble fingers, and are very small, but are packed with

genetic information about the baby. Genetic disorders and other abnormalities will be easily found within the information of the sample, to give you an idea of what conditions your child is likely to have or is susceptible to.

- **Noninvasive Prenatal Testing (NiPT)** - Noninvasive prenatal testing allows doctors to determine the likelihood of genetic disorders, but cannot confirm if the disorder is *actually* present. This test uses a basic blood draw, then identifies and analyzes the DNA that is found in Mom's blood that originates from the baby's placenta, to screen for chromosomal abnormalities. If there is anything that raises a red flag, your medical practitioner may then recommend further screening to determine if there are genetic abnormalities present.
- **Nuchal Translucency Screening (NT)** - Nuchal translucency screening is a routine procedure done with an ultrasound. Nearing the end of the first trimester, the ultrasound is used to determine the likelihood of chromosomal abnormalities or congenital heart conditions, but cannot be used to diagnose the conditions. The ultrasound measures a transparent area that sits at the base of the baby's neck called the nuchal fold, to see how much fluid has been retained in that area. If there is a larger amount of fluid built up in the area than average, it can indicate that the baby may be at a higher likelihood for congenital heart defect and chromosomal disorders. This screening is known to often result in false positives, so if you do get a concerning screening result, don't stress until other tests are done to confirm the findings.
- **Pap Smear** - A pap smear is likely to be done at a few points during the pregnancy, not only to check for sexually transmitted diseases, but to monitor any changes in the cervix that may indicate problems in the pregnancy. This might include the shape, appearance, and location of the cervix.
- **Rh Factor Testing** - Your Rh factor is the + or - that comes with your blood type. This is determined by whether or not your red blood cells carry the Rh factor protein on them; most people do have them, resulting in a positive blood type, like A

positive, B positive, etc. If you do not carry the protein, your blood type is A negative. This doesn't tend to have any impact on your daily life... until you're pregnant. If the parents have two different blood types, then the fetus can be conceived with a different blood type than Mom's. When that happens, she could be carrying antibodies that will attack the blood cells in the fetus, as they appear to be a foreign body. This testing helps determine if there needs to be any intervention to prevent the antibodies from disrupting the baby's development or affecting Mom's health.
- **Ultrasounds** - Ultrasounds are probably every parent's favorite regular screening, since it gives us an opportunity to see the baby-in-making. Ultrasounds will help your medical practitioner check on the baby's progress, as well as measure internal organs to make sure that there are no defects or problems. The ultrasound can also monitor placental positioning, cervix length, and the amount of fluids that are present within the womb, as well as giving you a sneak peak at the fetus in its natural habitat.
- **Urine Tests** - Urine testing will take place throughout the pregnancy. These are needed to test for a variety of issues like dehydration, urinary tract infections, sugar levels related to gestational diabetes, and proteins related to preeclampsia.

*Second Trimester*

- **Amniocentesis** - Having amniocentesis—otherwise known as an amnio—done will give you a plethora of genetic information. A needle is inserted into the uterus, and amniotic fluid is drawn into the syringe to be sent for genetic testing. Because it is gathered from the fluid that has been circulating through the fetus, it is rich with genetic information. This will give access to knowledge on all chromosomal conditions and potential deficits, so that parents can be better informed. As a nice cherry on top, it can also provide the sex of the baby, so if you don't want to know, make sure it's noted!
- **Glucose Screening** - The glucose screening is how medical practitioners will test for gestational diabetes. There are a few variations on the test depending on what your practitioner prefers, but they all boil down to a similar procedure. When Mom shows up for her appointment, she'll be given a glucose drink—usually flavored like orange soda, but flat and with the consistency of a light syrup. After some time, usually an hour, she'll have blood drawn to test the glucose levels in her blood. This will ensure that the pancreas is still producing insulin as it should be.
- **Quad Screen** - The quad screen is yet another blood test Mom will go through. This one will test four different chemicals that pass through her bloodstream as the blood cycles through her body and the placenta.
  - - Alpha-Fetoprotein (AFP), which is a protein produced by the baby.
  - - Estriol, a hormone in the estrogen family that is produced by both the baby and the placenta.
  - - Human chorionic gonadotropin (hCG), which is the pregnancy hormone that is also detected in urine during a positive pregnancy test. This hormone is produced by the placenta.
  - - Inhibin A, which is another hormone produced by the placenta.

- The quad screen will indicate whether your baby *may* have any neural tube defects or chromosomal conditions. This won't give a definitive answer, but will let doctors know if they need to do more in-depth testing.

*Third Trimester*

- **Biophysical Profile** - If the pregnancy is considered healthy and low risk, chances are that Mom won't need this one. The biophysical profile is another ultrasound that will focus on the baby's motion, breathing, the progress of their organs, and the amount of amniotic fluid. This profile screening is a way to check in on the baby to make sure that the pregnancy is progressing safely.
- **Group B Strep Test** - Group B strep is a bacteria that, while perfectly fine when found in adults, can lead to serious health complications if transmitted to the infant during birth. If Mom tests positive for this bacteria, she will be given a course of antibiotics to clear the infection before the baby is born.
- **Nonstress Test** - A nonstress test is administered for a variety of reasons: Mom may have preeclampsia or other gestational complications, the baby appears small in comparison to their gestational age, or you've surpassed your due date significantly, and it's time to check in on the baby. The baby will simply be monitored in a nonstress environment to ensure that everything is still in line with health parameters.

# CHAPTER 5
# FIRST TRIMESTER

 "Having a kid is like falling in love for the first time when you're 12, but every day."

– Mike Myers

THE FIRST TRIMESTER is a rollercoaster time period, but an exciting one! Trying to conceive is an emotional journey, so finally reaching the point where your partner is now forming your tiny life in her womb is something to celebrate. The first trimester is made up of the first 12 weeks of pregnancy, and can be a whirlwind time.

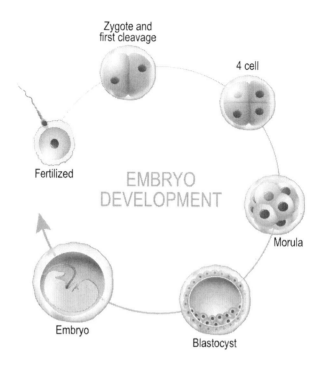

## WEEK 1 & 2

This time period actually starts at the first day of Mom's period, so the first couple of weeks are pretty uneventful in terms of gestation. The first week is the menstrual period where the lining of the uterus is shed from the past month, beginning the cycle of creating a fresh new uterine lining to support an implanted fertilized egg. As a matter of fact, the day you're looking for is the last day of the second week, approximately the 14th day of the cycle when the ovary releases the egg, hoping to be fertilized by some lucky sperm. This fertility window opens three to five days before ovulation, depending on Mom's typical cycle. Once the egg is fertilized, it'll be implanted, and you can consider yourselves pregnant!

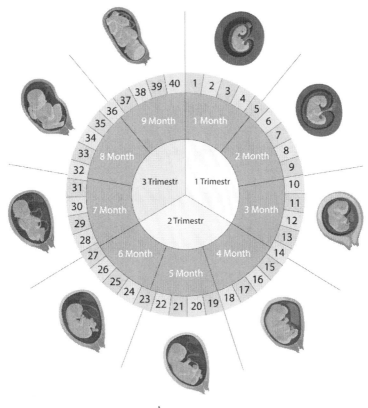

EMBRYO DEVELOPMENT

## WEEK 3

Most women don't know they're pregnant at this point, and most tests won't pick up the pregnancy at this point. There are rarely any symptoms at this point. Some might notice a tiny bit of spotting or the slightest bit of cramping, but otherwise, most people don't recognize any kind of change by week three. The earliest signs of pregnancy that might possibly occur is your partner's breasts being more tender or swollen, and she may have a heightened sense of smell. Some women may experience some nausea from the shifting hormones as well. Right now, your baby is a blastocyst, which is the tiniest little cluster of multiplying cells.

## WEEK 4

### How is the Baby?

This week, your future baby changes from a blastocyst to an embryo. Within the uterus, the amniotic sac and placenta that will protect your baby in utero are beginning to form. If you and your partner have been actively trying to get pregnant, this may be the point, right about the time  she should be missing her period, that the pregnancy should become visible on home pregnancy tests.

### How is Mom?

Typically, there aren't many symptoms at this point, but this will vary person to person. Some will experience some mild pressure in or around their uterus, or may see some implantation bleeding. Others may notice symptoms like tender breasts or feeling exhausted, but it's also just as normal to notice no symptoms at all! It's easy to mistake the earliest symptoms as an oncoming menstrual period. Of course, the rapidly rising rate of the pregnancy hormones may bring along some nausea or vomiting, but not every pregnancy comes with morning sickness. Symptoms will range per person, so don't jump at every sneeze or mood swing.

### How Can Dad Help?

First, bring home a pregnancy test! This is the ideal time to start testing, after all. Bear in mind that human chorionic gonadotropin (hCG), the hormone released by the placenta during pregnancy, will increase at different rates per person, so it's entirely possible to get a false negative or a very faint positive at this stage. If you do get that positive pregnancy test, it's time to make an appointment for prenatal care so that Mom and baby's health and progress can be tracked.

If your partner is experiencing any potential symptoms, treat it the same way you might help soothe period symptoms: warm compresses for cramping, ginger or ginger ale for the nausea, and caring for your partner's emotional state. If you're not sure what your partner really needs, communicate! They can tell you far better than the pages of a book, in terms of what they individually need to soothe discomfort.

If you have any major concerns about disorders like sickle cell disease and other genetic disorders, consider carrier screening. It's a simple saliva or blood test that can help you prepare if you know that yourself or your partner are carriers of any major disorders so that you can be prepared, if you so choose.

Finally, if you've gotten a positive on the pregnancy test, what your partner consumes now becomes important. Prenatal vitamins are a great thing to start now if they haven't been already. In terms of dietary needs this week, vitamin D and healthy fats are a great place to focus your energy. If she's struggling with getting the good leafy greens in due to nausea, hide them in fruit smoothies or blend them into pasta sauces. If your partner's nausea is making it difficult to eat, work with them to get them what they need.

## WEEK 5

*How is Baby?*

Right now, your baby looks like a tadpole. The nutrients Mom is giving the baby are helping it to form its nerve passageways; this includes the brain, spinal cord, and nerves, giving the baby the appearance of having a tail. The baby's gut, heart, and lungs are also starting to form this week. These crucial organs developing means that if Mom is usually a smoker or around smokers, she should be removing herself from that smoke exposure, as well as away from alcohol consumption. Caffeine consumption should be reduced to about one or two small cups of coffee in a day, since there isn't enough known about the effects of caffeine on the baby at this time.

### How is Mom?

If the pregnancy test from last week left you guessing, this week should give you something far more conclusive to go off of. Fatigue, tender breasts, nausea, and now needing to run to pee constantly are going to be the normal, expected symptoms your partner might experience. Hormones are climbing in your partner's body at an exceptional rate, so be patient with any hormonal mood swings that she may be experiencing. Food aversions may be starting to set in, making cooking and eating certain items seem impossible, so adjusting the food Mom is eating may be necessary.

### How Can Dad Help?

From here on out, if you have a cat, your pregnant partner should skip cleaning the litter box. This doesn't mean get rid of the cat, as some folk legends suggest. Dealing with litter boxes and gardening without gloves can contribute to contracting an infection called toxoplasmosis, which can harm both Mom and baby. Anywhere that outdoor cats might be using as a potty is generally good for Mom to avoid if possible, including uncovered sandboxes.

Some couples find that a pregnancy journal can be great to start at this time. This will give parents and child a way to look back on the pregnancy, and creates a keepsake for the child. It's also a great time to start talking about saving money for the baby, both for baby's arrival and their future.

## WEEK 6

### How is Baby?

Your baby's heart is working overtime! Right now, the baby's heart rate is double yours. Baby's little face is beginning to take shape, and may even be visible in an ultrasound. Their features may only show as small dark spots on their face at this point, but they're there! Even the baby's tongue and vocal cords are forming right now, along with the ears. It won't be long until the baby will be able to hear your voice through Mom's belly. Tiny arms and legs are also budding at this point, though your baby still looks a bit like a tadpole with a tail.

*How is Mom?*

Mom might be feeling a little more emotional right about now. This is all pretty new, so combining the hormonal changes with the physical changes, plus the stress and nerves that can come with knowing you're really pregnant, can create a melting pot of worry. Strange dreams might come with the subconscious stress that she may be feeling right now. Worries about the baby's health, how the balance of baby and work and social life will work, if you've got the finances in place, or if you'll be good parents can all pile up and reflect in her moods.

Physically, your partner is probably feeling the need to pee a lot more often. Blood is being pushed by rising levels of hCG to her pelvic area. Odd cravings may begin to develop, fatigue and morning sickness may be in full swing, and heartburn may start to rear its ugly head, thanks to hormones relaxing the band that typically keeps stomach acids where they belong. If that wasn't enough, many women begin experiencing headaches around this point, often related to not getting enough sleep, their cravings that might be loaded with sodium or MSG, stress, being around smoke, or other factors. Take the time to find the source of the headaches so that you can get rid of them effectively.

### How Can Dad Help?

Since you're still very early in the pregnancy, this is a great time to be educating yourselves in the foods that aren't safe to eat during pregnancy, or that aren't recommended to consume in high amounts. This includes foods like soft cheeses, overly processed meats, raw meats and fish, and some shellfish. Educating yourself ahead of time will mean making it easier to make a choice for food when you're out for a meal. There are lots of apps that can help you figure out if food is safe while on the go as well.

Regarding the health of Mom and baby, healthy snacks and taking short walks can be a great way to prevent the worst of the soreness that can set in from pregnancy down the road, especially if you make it a habit now. Otherwise, if your partner is showing signs of stress, offer a listening ear. Ask her if she just wants to be heard, or if she wants solutions; if she wants solutions, then you can begin looking realistically into whatever is worrying her. Otherwise, just hear her out and soothe her however works best for her, and let her know that she has your support. Do what you can to help her reduce stress if the hormones are running away with her. If there's a routine that she tends to enjoy to destress, like a warm—not hot! Extreme temperatures are bad for the baby!—bath or massage, set them up for her. Take the initiative, rather than waiting for her to ask for you to do something kind.

## WEEK 7

### How is Baby?

Your baby's brain is expanding like crazy this week! Roughly 100 new brain cells are generated per minute in this stage, since the energy of reproducing and growing is being focused on the head right now. The little buds that were the beginnings of arms and legs are developing more this week as well, but they still look like tiny paddles for now. Your baby's kidneys have also begun developing, and getting ready to start working on waste management; yes, the baby *does* pee in the womb!

*How is Mom?*

Mom's symptoms are probably fairly consistent with what she's been experiencing up to this point, except for the fact that she may have gone up a whole bra size by this point. Mom may already be experiencing the itching that comes along with stretching skin. She should build the habit early to be moisturizing areas like the hips, buttocks, breasts, legs, and belly to reduce the discomfort of stretching skin. There's also the issue of all the excess saliva. Saliva production goes wild thanks to those pregnancy hormones, as well as her acne going crazy. If Mom typically goes to the gym to work out, she only has a few more weeks where she can safely and comfortably work out her back, so she should definitely get in her exercises while she can!

*How Can Dad Help?*

For now, what you've been doing up to this point is what you should continue doing. Continue to offer support for the pregnancy symptoms that your partner is experiencing, listening to their worries, and communicating plans and ideas for the birth, even if it seems as though it's forever away. It can be a great idea to get a pulse on your relationship; making sure the foundations of your relationship are strong will ensure that you can both feel secure in your ability to parent and communicate with each other when things are difficult, due to sleep deprivation. It may even be fun to come up with name ideas, what your official pregnancy announcement will be, and discuss what you're excited about.

## WEEK 8

*How is Baby?*

This week, your baby is starting to move around, although it's incredibly unlikely for you or Mom to feel the movements at this point. These movements are happening as the baby's nerves develop, causing it to twitch and move unpredictably. Meanwhile, little features like lips, eyelids, and even a tiny baby nose are starting to form. The baby is growing very quickly right now, making it easier to see its shape in ultrasounds.

*How is Mom?*

Mom might be feeling the baby weight right now. While it isn't likely that she's showing yet, she's probably starting to put on a bit of weight; this is a good thing! It is crucial for her to be putting on weight throughout her pregnancy to support the baby as best she can. Having a steady supply of fruit available will also supply the fibre she needs to combat the constipation that might be setting in around this time. Alongside the fruit, Mom should be staying well hydrated.

Fatigue is also normal at this stage; she may have barely done anything that day, and still feel like she needs a nap. This could be partly due to the crazy pregnancy dreams that she might be having, as well as the energy it takes to be making the baby. Finally, she may be noticing some changes in her vaginal discharge; it may be thickening into something that looks white and creamy. As long as the change isn't drastically altering the smell and color, it's perfectly normal. It is still safe to be having sex, despite the changes in the discharge. As long as the pregnancy is healthy and she can get into a comfortable position, the changes in her discharge won't affect her ability to enjoy some one-on-one affection!

*How Can Dad Help?*

Keep fresh fruit stocked in the house. Make sure it's something that she feels she can eat if she is experiencing morning sickness. Especially if she's having trouble getting her veggies to stay down, keeping a rainbow fruit assortment can mean still getting the nutrition she needs to support both herself and the growing baby. Regardless of the season, keep a bottle of sunscreen around. Pregnancy can bring on melasma, a condition that causes darker hyperpigmentation of the skin. Keeping the skin protected (yes, even during the winter!) can keep this from happening.

If you're a couple that does meal planning, Mom will benefit from having smaller, more frequent meals throughout the day. Even if she's still dealing with morning sickness, having something small available when she feels like she can eat will do wonders. Especially when combined with the fatigue that comes with pregnancy, small pre-made meals that she can quickly warm up if needed can help ensure that she's eating well for both her and baby.

## WEEK 9

*How is Baby?*

It's officially the third month of pregnancy! This is the final week that the baby is classified as an embryo, and will be moving on to its fetus stage next week. The baby's facial features, as well as tiny toes, knees, and elbows are formed and potentially visible in an ultrasound. If the baby is positioned in the right area, the heartbeat can even be heard during the ultrasound. Now that the baby is about an inch long, it'll be easier for an ultrasound technician to tell if you're having one baby, or multiples!

*How is Mom?*

Meanwhile, fatigue is probably kicking Mom's butt. Her body is working overtime to form the placenta that will surround and protect the baby, as well as getting baby the oxygen and nutrients that it needs to keep growing at a steady rate. Between the hormones, the fatigue, heartburn, sore breasts, and the weight gain as her uterus expands, she might be going through some hefty mood swings.

If there are any complications within the pregnancy, signs can start right around this time period. Issues like spotting and bleeding, excessive cramping in the lower back, and severe itching can all indicate that there may be something wrong.

*How Can Dad Help?*

For now, keep stocked up on those snacks! Keeping food down as much as possible will help Mom with the heartburn, while also keeping her and baby fed. If Mom is still feeling the fatigue, pick up the slack where she's struggling to keep up, and help her with the bigger tasks around the house. If you're looking to treat her, look into what spa treatments are available locally, and check that they are safe for pregnancy.

## WEEK 10

*How is Baby?*

Congratulations! Your embryo has officially graduated from embryo to fetus! Your baby is going through a bunch of new changes this week. You might even be able to get a firsthand look at it, as most doctors will schedule the first ultrasound between this week and next. The baby's forehead will probably look like it has a hump, since the brain is developing and starting to bulge forward. The baby's teeth are also starting to form and harden, attaching themselves to the jaw bone. Bones are also beginning to form and harden right now, and the baby can already bend and flex their tiny arms and legs. The baby's organs are also developing, such as stomach and kidneys. If the baby is a boy, he's already started producing testosterone.

*How is Mom?*

As for Mom, she's about to start showing if she isn't already. Her uterus has expanded enough to start seeing some rounding in her lower belly, depending on her height, build, and weight. This outwards push could mean feeling cramping in her lower abdomen, but there's no need to panic just yet! Round ligament pain—which is going to come from the ligaments that will do some of the major lifting as the baby grows—may be setting in due to stretching right about now. While some hardly notice them, other women find the pain can almost rival their menstrual cramps.

If Mom has been experiencing mood swings, they should be coming to an end in the next few weeks, but can likely return near the end of the pregnancy. She may find that she's dealing with excessive saliva production, veins becoming more visible, some level of constipation, and the constant feeling of needing to pee. All of this is normal, and comes with the territory of fluctuating hormones and the exhaustion of building a whole human from scratch. Considering how much the baby is growing right now, she should be staying on top of taking her vitamins, especially folic acid, vitamins A through E, and iron to help with the energy levels.

Mom's clothes might also be getting tight right about now. If she doesn't already have some, it may be time for her to get some maternity pants, or some other stretchy clothes that will grow with her. Don't go too crazy on them yet though; she's still got a long way to go in terms of her changing body.

*How Can Dad Help?*

If the first ultrasound is this week, celebrate and enjoy it with your partner. This is the first look you're getting at the being that will be your child, so cherish the moment as much as you can. You should also discuss with your partner if you'd like to have any potential screenings done. There are a variety to choose from, and they will let you know if your baby will have any special needs or conditions that could effect their quality of life.

It's also time to start considering your budget for baby's arrival. New babies are quite expensive, so now that you're nearing the end of the first trimester, talking about savings, work schedules, and the possibility of either of you being stay-at-home or work-from-home parent is important. It should also be on the radar to discuss maternity leave and/or paternity leave between the two of you, and with your respective employers. While you don't necessarily have to do it right now, your employer will need time to find a replacement for either of you while you're gone, as well as making the time for the appointments associated with pregnancy. In Mom's case, they may also have to adjust the type of work she's doing, so that she's not putting excessive strain on her body or exposing herself to dangerous chemicals.

## WEEK 11

*How is Baby?*

Baby is truly leaving their amphibian phase, and really embracing their new fetus stage. They're now moving about freely, doing somersaults, kicks, and stretches now that the body is starting to straighten out. Webbing that once connected the fingers and toes is now disappearing, and individual fingers and toes are visible and wiggling freely. On those fingers and toes, there are nascent nail beds, but don't worry, they won't be hardening into the nails we have for some time. They may be sharp, but they'll be fairly paper-like until after the baby is born. Even the baby's hair follicles are developing over their head and all over their body, so they can grow hair to help keep them warm when they make their entrance.

If your baby is a girl, this week her ovaries will develop. Regardless of gender, the external sex organs are beginning to develop, but they won't be distinguishable enough at this point to see clearly on an ultrasound if you're having a boy or a girl. While these organs are developing, other internal organs are starting to function. The pancreas, kidneys, and liver are all doing their jobs: making insulin, urine, and red blood cells respectively.

*How is Mom?*

Mom's first trimester symptoms should start tapering off at this point, only to be replaced by the second trimester symptoms. It'll be important for her to stay well hydrated to fend off constipation and leg cramping, even though it'll contribute to her needing the bathroom constantly. She may also be noticing some darkening in her skin; a line may become visible that runs through the center of her abdomen called linea nigra, as well as her areolas darkening. These color changes won't stick around forever. They typically disappear after the birth; they may linger during breastfeeding due to the hormones associated with nursing, but they'll eventually fade out and disappear.

She may also feel a little more stomach trouble, but in the form of gas and bloating. This arises from slowed digestion, thanks to those lovely hormone changes (they really are to blame for pretty much every discomfort at this point) and the shifting inside her body as the baby grows and the uterus expands. High-fiber foods and lots of water can help, as well as avoiding the foods that cause gas, if it's making her uncomfortable.

*How Can Dad Help?*

A babymoon is a great way to bond with your partner before the baby arrives. The second trimester is probably the ideal time if you want to travel a little bit, so start your planning now! The harsh symptoms of the first trimester are probably subsiding, and the third trimester tends to get more uncomfortable. Meanwhile, the second trimester is usually the point where most women get to really enjoy their pregnancy, so this is the best time to go on a special little vacation if you can.

# WEEK 12

*How is Baby?*

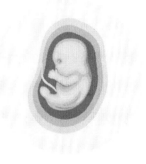

It's the final week of the first trimester! You're a third of the way to becoming new parents now—how does it feel? If you and your partner have been worried about miscarriage, reaching the 12-week mark is a great sign, since the chances of miscarriage drop significantly now.

At this point, all of your baby's major organs have formed, and from this point on, the baby will be putting all of its energy into developing and growing all its parts. The organs are all functioning, with its bone marrow now working on creating white blood cells, and the intestines are getting in practice with working food through them. Right now, the baby is getting a start on making meconium, which will be their first poop. This is mostly made up of cells, bile, and various types of proteins and fats that get processed through their organs. The baby can now do things like clench their fists, and is getting way more active.

While not common, some women might feel a little flutter of movement in her womb, commonly mistaken for gas rolling through the intestines. It's not likely that you'll feel anything with your hand on her belly, but that time is coming soon!

*How is Mom?*

While most of the harsher symptoms of the first trimester should be slowing down, hormones are doing new things in Mom's body. One of these hormones, progesterone, can start causing dizziness, thanks to its ability to restrict and dilate blood vessels. This change in the blood vessels can even make her feel short of breath, so if dizziness or having a tough time breathing kicks in, she should take a seat and rest for a while. If she's wearing tight clothing, it can help to loosen them up and take a moments rest to gather herself. Progesterone can also drastically affect her libido, but which direction is highly dependent on the person. Some will feel their libido sink entirely due to the hormone shift, while others might not be able to get enough.

*How Can Dad Help?*

If you haven't already, the 16th-week ultrasound should be scheduled. Otherwise, keep the pregnancy-safe foods stocked up, and roll with the changes in Mom's libido. Especially if her libido is down, don't take it personally; she isn't in control of her hormones, and it's not likely anything to do with you. If you have any concerns, communicate with her about them. There isn't anything wrong with checking in to make sure that the relationship is stable, and that she's doing well, mentally. If the stress and anxiety that come with depression are really settling in, encourage her to speak with a therapist to help alleviate these worries from her mind.

# CHAPTER 6
# SECOND TRIMESTER

 "Words can not express the joy of new life." — Hermann Hesse

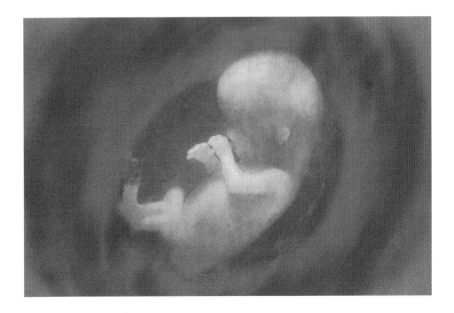

WELCOME TO THE SECOND TRIMESTER! The second trimester is where the funnest parts of pregnancy often take place, so

enjoy it as much as you can. Now that Mom's worst symptoms should be starting to alleviate, you get to look forward to the amazing growing belly, the kicks, the gender reveal (if you want to know what you're having,) and all kinds of other cool moments in the pregnancy.

## WEEK 13

*How is Baby?*

Baby is working on their vocal cords this week, getting ready for you to hear their little voice. In the vicinity, the eyelids are present, but they're still fused closed to protect their delicate eyes. They will stay this way for a while still. At the same time, bones within the skull, as well as the longer bones of the body and teeth, are becoming more dense and are hardening. This will help the baby to move more effectively, and they may even start sucking on their thumb.

Baby's intestines are also moving into the area that they will be staying long term. Before this week, the intestines were actually tucked away within the umbilical cord, but they'll start their journey into the abdominal cavity while they work on storing up their first poops. This comes from the fact that the baby is now swallowing amniotic fluid, cycling the fluid through their urinary and digestive system.

*How is Mom?*

Mom's appetite should return in full force right about now, which will help with the weight that she should be putting on to support the pregnancy. She's likely enjoying the break from morning sickness, and may even be sleeping a little bit better as she adjusts to the hormone changes that she's been experiencing. This can mean that she has a lot more energy than she had over the last few months.

While some symptoms are alleviating, she may still be experiencing some of the more pesky ones, like heartburn and cramping, thanks to the round ligaments stretching out. Constipation and indigestion can still be lingering, meaning she needs to keep her water intake up, and keep eating smaller, more frequent meals with a good level of fiber. Apart from this, she still needs to be taking her prenatal vitamins. Folic acid, calcium, protein, and iron are all important during this stage of the pregnancy.

An increase in vaginal discharge is also fairly standard at this point, and may not be such a bad thing if she's been experiencing a heightened libido. On the other hand, she may also be dealing with new levels of congestion, which some women experience thanks to those lovely pregnancy hormones. If she happens to be dealing with a cold at the same time, she'll need to go the all-natural route, since most cold medications aren't pregnancy safe.

*How Can Dad Help?*

For now, embrace the window of relief that your partner is feeling; while her libido may be up, certainly enjoy it, but get out of bed and go enjoy yourselves doing pregnancy-safe activities that you previously enjoyed doing together. Whether it's going for walks and hikes, swimming, doing something artsy, or enjoying some restaurant food instead of home cooking, enjoy the time you have where it's just the two of you. Just be careful if she's still experiencing some of the dizziness and headaches that can sometimes come with pregnancy. It's great if she has a lot more energy, but be careful about going too hard on the physical endeavors so she doesn't risk fall or injury. On the topic of food, if the morning sickness and food aversions are settling down, enjoy cooking and eating together, especially the foods that she has regained an appetite for.

## WEEK 14

*How is Baby?*

This week, the baby's face is getting a serious workout. Because of the development going on in the brain, the baby's face is making all kinds of expressions, flexing the tiny muscles that will eventually help them smile and frown. Those spurts of movement, thanks to their developing brain, also contribute to the baby starting to move, kick, punch, and stretch more these days, even if you can't *quite* feel them at it yet.

They're also slowly growing more of the fuzzy hair that covers them from head to toe, and it will slowly become more pronounced around the head, eyebrows, and eyelashes. The hair that will grow to cover the baby's body is called lanugo, which is very fine. Think of a tiny baby otter with a thin coating of fuzzy, soft hair covering them for warmth. The baby will likely hold onto that lanugo until they're born, when they'll shed the fuzz and opt for clothes and smooth baby skin. The purpose of the lanugo is to keep the baby warm while their baby fat comes in. While the baby's body is developing, the priority isn't necessarily putting on baby fat, but putting the energy towards growing and developing muscles, bones, and organs.

Possibly the most exciting development that your baby is going through right now is the full formation of external sex organs. For now, it might be a bit difficult to see in the ultrasounds, since baby is still quite small—roughly the size of your fist. In just a few more weeks, it will become much easier to see on the ultrasound if you're hoping to know your little one's gender.

*How is Mom?*

This is likely a very exciting time if Mom hasn't been showing a whole lot up to this point. By week 14, the baby bump is well underway for most, so if she's not seeing it as much as she'd like, that bump will be popping up in no time! She's also going to be enjoying some shinier and even thicker hair. If she already had thick hair to begin with, she may consider getting it thinned out at some point just for the sake of comfort. Her nails may also be growing in stronger and longer than before; there are upsides to the pregnancy hormones after all.

Despite feeling better, the round ligament pains might be coming in with a vengeance right now, since she's starting to show more. Her body knows it's about to expand a lot more around the middle, so it's doing everything to get those ligaments ready. If she hasn't already been working on strengthening her pelvic floor muscles, some pelvic muscle exercises will help her in the long run as the baby grows. If the round ligament pains are really bothering her, a warm or cool compress can help. If they're really uncomfortable, maternity belts and spider tapes can help to relieve some of the pain, as well as gentle massage.

Finally, she may be experiencing something sort of strange that nobody tends to mention; bleeding gums. Pregnancy gingivitis isn't uncommon, and can come about because of hormone changes, as well as being increasingly sensitive to bacteria. Increasing the amount that she's brushing and flossing can be a big help in minimizing the effects of pregnancy gingivitis, as well as still going on regular dentist visits. Especially after dealing with morning sickness, visiting a dentist can help negate any long-term effects that her teeth deal with during pregnancy.

*How Can Dad Help?*

Both of you should be working hard to stay healthy right about now. Depending on what time of the year you and your partner conceived, you may be going through cold and flu season right about now. Washing hands, using hand sanitizer, and generally keeping a distance from sick people should be high on both of your priority lists. Right now, Mom's immune system is way more susceptible to illness, so commit yourself to germ and virus destruction. If you happen to catch something, keep your distance and maybe sleep in the guest room or on the couch. If Mom happens to catch a cold or other virus, get her to a doctor who can prescribe pregnancy-appropriate antibiotics or medications.

## WEEK 15

*How is Baby?*

If you could see into baby's little home in the uterus this week, they might look like something out of a sci-fi movie. The baby's skin is formed, but for now, it's still very thin, meaning that you could easily see through it and peek at all of its blood vessels. The skeleton is continuing to harden, and is now hard enough that, if you were to x-ray your baby (not recommended to do so though, as the radiation is not good for a fetus), you would be able to see a little skeleton forming. As the skull hardens, the eyes and ears are migrating into the places they should be. Soon, they will arrive where they are going to be staying, and your baby's face will be officially formed.

The baby is also poking its tongue out these days, tasting the amniotic fluid. That may sound strange, but if you had brand new taste buds, you'd probably be pretty excited to taste everything in your environment too! The most interesting thing is, in a way, the baby can taste what Mom eats through the amniotic fluid. It's not in the way you think; if she eats a carrot, the amniotic fluid doesn't become carrot flavored. The compounds within the foods, like amino acids, proteins, glucose, fats, and minerals can make their way into the amniotic fluid, giving the baby a sense of the food that is available in the outside world. If Mom eats a shawarma, the baby may not taste exactly what a shawarma is like, but they can still taste some of the compounds that give food their flavor. A fetus in utero can even respond to presumably favorite or disliked foods, depending on their reactions to certain foods.

The baby is getting plenty of practice in for when they make their grand arrival into the world. They've started not only doing fetal aerobics, but also practicing skills like sucking, swallowing, and even breathing so that their reflexes and muscles are prepared for life outside of the womb. These fetal aerobics of punching, kicking, rolling, and stretching may mean that very, very soon, Mom might be feeling the baby move, if she hasn't already. You might struggle to feel the baby with your hand on her belly, but internally, most women compare the early feeling of the kicks to popcorn popping in the belly, lots of gas moving through the belly, or someone flicking her from the inside.

*How is Mom?*

Physically, the symptoms Mom has been experiencing going into trimester number two should still continue. Bouts of round ligament pain are standard, and of course, paying extra attention to her teeth and gums right now is a must. While she's coping with her pregnancy symptoms, her weight gain should be fairly steady; roughly four pounds or about 2 kilograms a month is the average. It's okay if she's a little above or below the average monthly net weight gain. Every Mom is different, with varying metabolisms and body types, so if her weight gain is off by a few pounds, it's nothing to worry too much about, unless otherwise indicated by the doctor.

Of the stranger pregnancy symptoms, Mom may also be dealing with nosebleeds. The hormones that have caused her to feel congested, combined with all of the extra blood that is in her body these days, are to blame for this one. These hormones are going to make her nasal cavities far more sensitive, and may thin the membranes just enough that nosebleeds can happen. This is normal, but if it seems that she's bleeding an awful lot and you're concerned, you can always talk to your medical practitioner just to make sure everything is okay.

Does Mom seem a little more disorganized lately? This may be a sign of "pregnancy brain" kicking in. Mom's brain actually does change during pregnancy, to the point that in the third trimester, the brain will lose brain cell volume. This is temporary, but it's the reason that Mom starts forgetting appointments, misplaces things more often than she used to, and may even forget what she's talking about mid sentence. This early into pregnancy brain, it's less to do with decreased brain cell volume, and more to do with the combination of altered sleeping, hormones raging, and an overall feeling of brain fog. If she's struggling with pregnancy brain, it may be a good idea to start using her calendar and notes apps on her phone (provided that she can keep track of where she left it.)

*How Can Dad Help?*

There are two important things to discuss right now; one, if your partner is at risk for preeclampsia, she should speak to her medical practitioner if a low dose or baby aspirin will be appropriate for her to take, to help lower the risk of high blood pressure setting in. Two, it's time to discuss whether or not amnio, short for amniocentesis, is a test that you would want to pursue. Right now, the amniotic fluid is packed full of genetic information about the baby. Amniotic fluid can be extracted for testing, but it doesn't need to be done for every pregnancy. This is ideal particularly when there is a family history of health conditions like sickle cell anemia, Downs Syndrome, or Tay-Sachs, among a variety of other disorders. It may also be recommended if other screening procedures have come back with abnormalities. If you have a relatively healthy family history and your screenings up to this point have all pointed to a healthy baby, amnio may not have to be on the table at all, but it's definitely worth the discussion. The plus side if you do decide to go for an amnio is that, with all that genetic information, they can determine the gender of the baby genetically, if you're really antsy to find out what you're having.

It's also time to decide if you want to pursue a birthing class. These classes often take about eight to twelve weeks to cover, so if it's on the priority list for you, it's time to start looking into classes near you. These classes will provide you with the knowledge and practical skills necessary to help you be a supportive partner to the best of your ability when the time comes, and for Mom to be prepared for what she's about to endure.

## WEEK 16

*How is Baby?*

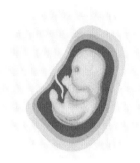

Baby's eyes and ears are beginning to function! Despite the eyelids still being fused shut, the baby can now shift its eyes back and forth, registering and responding to light sources. Within the baby's ears, the bones that help us to hear are settling into place and picking up on sound vibrations. The sounds are likely pretty muffled, but now the baby can pick up on the sounds of voices, music, and your pets if you have any.

The baby is also preparing for some pretty major growth spurts. Over the coming weeks, baby will double in size from where they are now. Everything is growing at an incredible pace; their heart is pumping up to 25 quarts of blood every day, the tissues of lungs and other organs are developing, the kidneys, pancreas, liver, and other digestive organs have begun to function, and their hair and nails are really coming into their own.

*How is Mom?*

Now that Mom's belly is really starting to grow, she may be starting to feel itchy where the skin is expanding. Stretch marks aren't avoidable if she's genetically predisposed to them, but she can make them a little better by slathering on a really good hydrating lotion or oil. That expanding belly means she may need to go shopping for some new maternity wear, if she hasn't already. The belly growing also means that back pain is going to be on the rise. Instead of laying out on the couch, which will only provide temporary relief, doing things like stretching and prenatal yoga can be helpful in strengthening and stretching those muscles to provide some relief and support as the belly keeps growing.

Pregnancy hormones are also bringing some positives and negatives to the table right now. On one hand, Mom may be experiencing some itchy, dry eyes with a side of pregnancy brain, but on the other, the hormones are bringing on the pregnancy glow. Her skin is clearing up, and maybe she's having to do less with her skin routine to look and feel the best she has this entire pregnancy. As long as she's using pregnancy-safe products, she can keep that glow going.

*How Can Dad Help?*

Now that Mom's belly is growing pretty significantly, she's going to have to adjust how she sleeps. While you may love a good cuddle before going to sleep, she may need to get comfortable in new side positions. As her belly keeps growing, help her by positioning pillows around her; one under the belly can provide support and pain relief, as well as one behind the back and between her knees.

Since baby is starting to see and hear, now you can start joining Mom on the fun of experiencing the baby. If the baby has reached the point where you're able to feel the little kicks, you can start playing with the baby; if you lay your ear on Mom's belly, you can sometimes hear the baby's movements and tiny sounds, and if you direct a flashlight onto her belly, the baby may actually respond by moving away from the light. Talking to the baby is also a great way to bond, and get the baby used to your voice before they're even born. Doing things like reading them stories, telling baby about your day, or just generally chatting with Mom with your head by her belly are all nice ways to have those bonding moments before the baby is ever born.

## WEEK 17

*How is Baby?*

Baby's heartbeat is double the rate of ours, about 140-150 beats a minute. The heartbeat is becoming more steady as their body becomes more regulated in the usage of its organs. As the organs become more regulated, the practice the baby has been getting has been slowly making it a champ at swallowing amniotic fluid and sucking its thumb. By the time the baby is born, eating and suckling will be second nature. This week, the baby's hearing is developing even more, so they'll better hear your voice or music you might play for them. They're also steadily putting on the baby fat that will keep them warm, not to mention squishy and cute, once they emerge into the world. Soon enough, their skin won't be so translucent. This is also the point when the baby really becomes their individual self, developing tiny fingerprints on their fingers and toes.

*How is Mom?*

While some of the strange pregnancy dreams may have begun in early pregnancy, they only get stranger as the hormones start to alter the brain. That's not the only sleep change she'll deal with though (this will mostly affect you); snoring. Get a humidifier into the room, and encourage Mom to sleep on her side so that you can catch some rest too.

Mom is really going to have to step up her stretching, to prevent and relieve sciatic pain. This nerve starts in the lower back, and runs downwards through the buttocks, legs, and ankles. As her belly grows and creates a deeper curve in her lower back, she may find that the sciatic nerve is pinched, so getting a warm compress on the area and following it up with prenatal back stretches can go a long way in relieving that pain.

This is also roughly the point that stretch marks start to appear over the belly, boobs, legs, and/or bum. Mom has been putting on weight fairly quickly, and some of the itchiness that she's experiencing is her skin trying to keep up with the rapid stretching of her skin. Lotions and moisturizing oils help to reduce the itchiness all over, and can help to prevent some of the additional stretch marks that come about.

*How Can Dad Help?*

Getting excited to meet the baby? Within the next few weeks, you should be seeing the gender in the ultrasound, usually between the 18 and 20-week scans. There's no better time to start talking about baby names, if you haven't chosen one already.

You may also have to become the tummy referee. Once Mom starts showing, people tend to think that it's no problem to reach over and start touching her belly. Especially when she's already itchy and sore among her other pregnancy symptoms, having someone constantly touching her belly without asking can't be the most pleasant. Be ready to subtly protect the belly if Mom is feeling uncomfortable; even if it's just getting your hand to her belly before the person can start touching, it can help enforce the boundary of "please don't touch Mom without permission."

## WEEK 18

*How is Baby?*

Your baby is starting to take shape, and really look like the baby that will be born. Their ears have found their forever home on the sides of the baby's head, and even more exciting, the baby's sex organs are in place and fully formed. This means that on your next ultrasound appointment, you very well could be finding out the gender of your baby! When looking at the ultrasound, the baby might still be hiding that knowledge with the way they've positioned themselves, but a surefire way to know what you're having is really peering in on the shapes. A baby girl will have what looks like three lines on the ultrasound, whereas a baby boy will look familiar to Dad, as it's pretty clearly an external organ sticking up.

Not so obvious on an ultrasound is the baby's other major development this week: their developing nervous system. In order for impulses to be transferred through the nervous system, to our brain, and then back out to produce our reactions, our nerves need a coating of myelin, which is like a slick fat coating on the nerve pathways to help the messages travel as quickly as possible through the nervous system. This myelin coating is developing this week, so hopefully your baby will develop some lightning-fast reflexes some day.

Finally, baby has learned a new trick this week; when they're tired, they now yawn. You might even catch a peek at their tiny yawn in the ultrasound!

*How is Mom?*

For now, most of Mom's symptoms are more or less the same as they have been. Some swollen feet after a long day standing, sore back, maybe some congestion, and the other typical symptoms that she's been feeling up to this point. There are a couple new ones that might be presenting themselves around this time though; one, she may start feeling a little unsteady. Not dizzy, but off balance, since the growing baby is throwing off her center of gravity, making her a little more clumsy than usual. Two, she might be getting quite the appetite these days. Specific food cravings and an insatiable hunger that seem to want to consume absolutely everything in sight is pretty normal.

### *How Can Dad Help?*

Getting in with a pediatrician can take a long time. This is the ideal time to find the pediatrician who will be looking after your little one after they arrive, since meeting doctors and waiting lists can take a while, depending on where you are. The pediatrician will likely be coming in to meet the baby within the first day or two of being born, so it's best to already have someone lined up sooner than later.

If Mom is struggling with the effects of relaxin, she may be due for a pregnancy massage. Relaxin is a hormone that does exactly what it sounds like; it relaxes the joints and ligaments to allow for Mom's body to expand for baby, and start repositioning for when the big day comes. If she's really sore and struggling, there are some prenatal massages that can be done in various spas and massage centers that accommodate for the growing belly, as well as restrictions on heat and types of oils not safe for a pregnant person.

Finally, it's also time to start considering maternity leave, and discussing when Mom will be putting in her paperwork to take leave. It's important to give her employer plenty of time to figure out staffing, and also to give your employer time as well if you'll be taking any amount of leave to help with the baby and Mom's recovery.

## WEEK 19

*How is Baby?*

Baby is now in sensory overdrive. The nerves that were developing over the last week have now given the baby a stronger sense of taste, smell, hearing, touch, and sight, so they're experiencing the womb in a whole new way. Baby's lungs are also continuing their development, and will continue to do so until the final weeks of pregnancy, when they'll be mature enough to function on their own.

In new developments, baby is forming a new layer that will cover up their skin. You know how your fingers and toes look when you've been sitting in water for a long time? The new wax-like coating, called vernix caseosa, will cover up the baby's sensitive skin so that your baby doesn't exit the womb looking more like a prune than a baby. This waxy, almost cheese-like substance does start to come off towards the end of the pregnancy, but babies born early may still be sporting their waxy coat.

*How is Mom?*

Mom is most likely pretty achy right now. Leg cramps, back aches, and swelling in the feet, hands, and maybe even legs have become her norm these days, which isn't likely to be the most comfortable thing in the world. The plus side is that baby is moving on a regular basis now, and it's pretty amazing to experience. She's probably finding it pretty difficult to get comfortable, and unfortunately it's not going to get much better until the baby arrives. Pillows are about to become her best friend.

She's also going to have to be on the lookout for yeast infections. Unfortunately, pregnant women can be prone to them, and from this stage of the pregnancy and going forward, they're even harder to treat and get under control. If she's showing symptoms, it's time to talk to her medical provider for a pregnancy-safe option to resolve the infection before it gets out of control.

*How Can Dad Help?*

For now, just do what you can to help keep her comfortable, which is going to be pretty difficult to do at some points. If she's hungry, try to (gently!) make recommendations for healthy greens, fiber, and lots of water. If you were a kid that loved to build pillow forts when you were young, use those skills to help your pregnant partner find comfort if at all possible, and otherwise, just give her an ear to voice her excitement and concerns. If you have any skills in massage, a foot rub or back rub will also go a long way from here on out.

## WEEK 20

*How is Baby?*

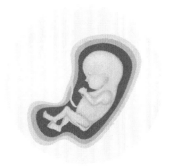

So far, baby is practicing their sucking and swallowing, and working towards perfecting their organs. They're also enjoying their new senses, and likely becoming much more active. Their organs are in place and functioning, so from here on out, they're going to be developing their organs and reflexes so that they're ready to use once the baby is out in the world.

*How is Mom?*

Mom is officially halfway through her pregnancy, so she may be celebrating that she's completed half the journey. In a few weeks, she'll be reaching the third trimester, so that end stretch is probably looking really sweet to her right about now! You may have noticed something new about her belly this week; her 'innie' belly button may have 'popped' and is now an 'outie.' This is normal, and her belly button will return to normal after she delivers.

Otherwise, Mom is likely going through a rotation of feeling restless and exhausted, and spurts of high energy. Those energy levels will probably dip in the third trimester though, so if she has anything she wants to get done for the baby, it should probably get started up about now. Some of the fatigue may be coming from depleted iron levels, so if she hasn't been using an iron supplement, she may benefit from starting one now.

## *How Can Dad Help?*

This is usually a good time to put together the baby registry if you and your partner haven't already, and time to talk about what is the preferred baby shower style for Mom. If you are planning to do it Jack and Jill style, or if you prefer to do them separately, it's time to discuss with each other first, and then family and friends can be called upon to get everything arranged.

If you haven't already talked about it, it may also be time to look into where Mom wants to give birth. It's important that Mom is comfortable when she's giving birth, so it's time to start figuring out the details and setting plans into motion so that she can get to where she wants to be once labor begins.

## WEEK 21

*How is Baby?*

Baby is becoming far more coordinated these days, doing a lot more flexing, stretching, kicking, and even playing with the umbilical cord. Despite the fact that it may seem like the baby never stops moving, they're actually beginning to sleep as much as a newborn.

*How is Mom?*

Stretch marks, soreness, and restlessness aside, Mom might be feeling some anxiety right now. Feeling the baby kick is a wonderful feeling, but it may be setting in that this is really happening; in about 19 weeks, there's going to be a tiny life that you two will be taking care of.

Braxton-Hicks contractions may be starting soon. Think of them as practice contractions. They'll be irregular, and pretty inconsistent throughout the remainder of the pregnancy. They can definitely be alarming the first few times Mom experiences them, since they seem to come on out of nowhere, and they might gradually become stronger as she gets closer to delivery day.

Mom might need to get herself some nursing pads soon. Her breasts are deep in their preparations for nursing the baby, so Mom might experience some leaking in the coming weeks.

*How Can Dad Help?*

Keep on supporting as you have been for now. If you've started birth prep classes, use some of the breathing techniques that you're learning to help Mom get through the Braxton-Hicks contractions.

## WEEK 22

*How is Baby?*

Baby's new favorite activity right now is grabbing at everything; their nose, their ears, and the umbilical cord. They're still developing their senses, and listening to Mom's heartbeat, digestion, and voice, as well as yours! They're becoming even more responsive to light, so feel free to play with them (as much as Mom has the patience for.) The baby's hair is also growing in right now, but there's no way to know just how much they'll have come their birthday.

*How is Mom?*

The hormones that were giving Mom her lush hair and long, strong nails are now working against her. The hair growth is now extending beyond her head, and probably growing thicker pretty much everywhere else. She'll have to be aware of how she typically removes hair if she chooses to; it's getting a lot harder for her to bend to shave, and some methods of hair removal, like lasers, bleach, and other chemicals are better to avoid during pregnancy. She may also experience her nails getting more brittle these days, and her once-glowing skin is now starting to break out, thanks to extra oil production. She may need to switch up her skin care products to reduce oil, and offer better moisturization.

*How Can Dad Help?*

Your focus going forward is going to center mostly on keeping Mom comfortable, and helping her to relax. Stay engaged with her needs, and help where you can. Pillows, healthy comfort foods, and a listening ear are going to be some of your best tools, along with foot and back rubs.

## WEEK 23

*How is Baby?*

Baby's skin is starting to sag, almost like an ill-fitting suit. Luckily, their skin will be filling out soon, since the skin is developing faster than the baby fat. The skin may be developing a nice rosy hue as well, all thanks to the blood vessels that are developing just under the surface of the skin. While their skeleton and organs might be visible through their skin right now, the fat stores will fill in soon enough so Mom gives birth to a healthy, chubby cutie.

*How is Mom?*

For now, Mom's symptoms are likely at a plateau; she's not really developing any new symptoms, but they're not going away either. If she needs something fun to boost her spirits and help her feel better, she should consider a dance class; it's great for developing the support muscles that help her alleviate pain, keep her weight gain in its healthiest range, and is great for her mental health. A bonus is that the baby will be able to feel her dancing, and may move along with her!

*How Can Dad Help?*

Keep on helping in Mom's relaxation, and help her in tackling the issues that may be stressing her out. At some point, you may need childcare for when Mom goes back to work. Much like pediatricians, daycares and sitters may have long wait lists, so it's best to get onto finding one sooner than later.

## WEEK 24

*How is Baby?*

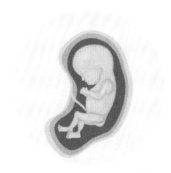

At the moment, baby is looking very white. The hair from their head to their toes is completely without pigment right now, so it's all very white. Pigment will come in eventually, but for now, the color of baby's hair and eyes is up in the air. While the baby is waiting for that pigment, they're slowly packing on baby fat.

Now that the baby's hearing is getting better, play some music or sing for them! When a baby hears a song frequently in utero, they may associate it to being a comfort after they're born, so pick a song to sing or play that you feel will be a good comfort for the baby, and won't drive Mom and Dad up the wall right away.

*How is Mom?*

Pregnancy hormones strike again. In this case, it's coming in the form of numbness and pain through the wrists and hands; good ol' carpal tunnel syndrome. If Mom is experiencing carpal tunnel, getting good wrist braces—as well as avoiding sleeping on her hands and keeping them elevated when lying down to rest—will help. While typical carpal tunnel is associated with repetitive motion in the wrists, pregnancy carpal tunnel comes from fluids collecting in the extremities that are putting pressure on the nerves. Luckily, Mom isn't likely to need surgery for her carpal tunnel, as it usually goes away with giving birth.

Mom might also be struck with some odd symptoms like skin tags, or her palms and soles of her feet may become red and itchy. These are normal symptoms for this stage of pregnancy, but in rare cases it may be an indicator of a disorder called cholestasis of pregnancy. This is related to bile production within the gallbladder being slowed or stopped thanks to the pregnancy, but it's highly uncommon. If Mom is dealing with redness and itchiness, and tests negative for cholestasis of pregnancy, the only real cure for it is delivery, so she should avoid things that make it worse, like long hot showers or doing dishes without rubber gloves on. Sometimes a soak in cold water can provide some relief.

*How Can Dad Help?*

Mom's glucose screening is probably this week, where they'll check for gestational diabetes. Support her through the appointment, and otherwise focus on soothing her worries and discomfort. You're likely becoming quite the pro at that by this point. It can also help to educate yourself on the signs of preterm labor, just in case. It's better to be prepared with the knowledge and not need it, versus not having the knowledge and having no idea what is happening or what to do.

## WEEK 25

*How is Baby?*

Baby's lungs will be developing through the rest of the pregnancy, but right now, they're using their nose more to figure out breathing. Of course, there's no air in the womb, but they're going to be breathing in amniotic fluid, as well as working on their sense of smell. This comes thanks to the amino acids, proteins, and other minerals imparted by Mom's food, so the baby will have an idea of what their parents eat on a regular basis. If baby is growing a good head of hair, you may be able to see the texture of the hair in the next ultrasound. Otherwise, baby is steadily putting on more weight in preparation for their big arrival.

*How is Mom?*

Swollen varicose veins and spider veins aren't uncommon in pregnancy. Unfortunately, this also applies to the veins within the rectum, resulting in hemorrhoids in roughly half of pregnant women. If this is the case for Mom, she should focus on getting both fiber and extra water. If constipation is plaguing her, she should get a short stool to put her feet on while on the toilet, to help move things along a little easier.

Round ligament pain may be coming and going for some, as well as a condition called symphysis pubis dysfunction. The hormone relaxin is to blame for this one, since it's relaxing the ligaments and joints throughout the pelvis. An exercise ball and working on the pelvic floor muscles can help relieve the worst of the symptoms of symphysis pubis dysfunction.

Hormones can also be affecting her eyesight right now. If she's always had perfect vision, she might find herself squinting to see things that she never would have had issue with before. While the change in eyesight can sometimes be permanent, it typically returns to normal after having the baby.

Finally, if anxiety and depression are ramping up right now, Mom should consider speaking to her doctor about it. The stress of pregnancy symptoms making her feel crappy, topped with worries of the future, plus the compounding hormones can really be getting to Mom right now. She should be speaking to her doctor or therapist, as well as her support system of family and friends to help reduce the stress, and hopefully have a happier pregnancy.

*How Can Dad Help?*

This is preparation time! If you've found a pediatrician, start talking to them about recommendations of what to buy and not buy for baby. You may also want to start rearranging your kitchen to make meal prep a little easier and quicker, and start getting used to meals that offer nutrition, while also being quick and easy to make while minimizing clean up. When baby arrives, both you and Mom likely won't be too interested in cooking major meals, so start figuring out meals now that will be easily made when you're both sleep deprived and lacking in energy.

## WEEK 26

*How is Baby?*

Those little eyes that have been fused shut for months are finally starting to open! They're complete with lovely eyelashes as baby checks out their environment that they've been floating around in for the last two trimesters.

Baby's brain activity is also bumping up this week, so they're starting to actually react, compared to their earlier responses coming from nerves firing off during brain development. Their startle reflex is coming in, among other reflexes, that will help the baby to figure out the world when they arrive.

*How is Mom?*

Heartburn, restless leg syndrome, cramping, back aches, and a squirming baby are probably making it impossible for Mom to sleep these days. Insomnia normally sets in right about now, but luckily,

Mom is going into the home stretch. Clumsiness, migraines, and pregnancy brain are likely all on the rise, thanks to the hormones and lack of sleep. Mom is probably feeling like she should just move into the bathroom by now, with a karate-kicking baby pummeling her bladder. Only 14 weeks left before she starts feeling more like herself!

## *How Can Dad Help?*

If gifts are starting to roll in from family and friends, it's time to start going through them to make sure that they'll be safe for the baby. Especially secondhand items should be checked over thoroughly to make sure they're meeting today's safety requirements. If the items are deemed safe and secure for your baby, it's a great time to get everything set up in the baby's nursery. You can also go through the house and consider what will need to be babyproofed and moved around.

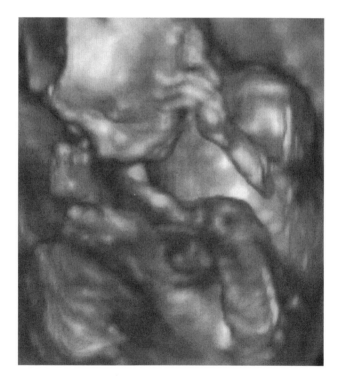

# CHAPTER 7
# THIRD TRIMESTER

> "Life is a flame that is always burning itself out, but it catches fire again every time a child is born." — George Bernard Shaw

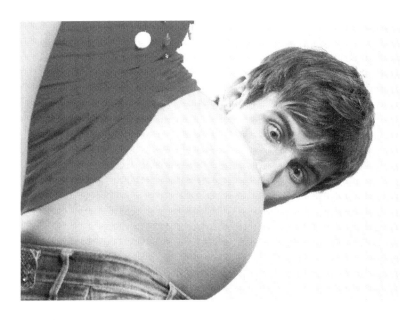

WELCOME to the final stretch of pregnancy! 13 short weeks from now, you'll likely be holding your baby, and setting off on your new lifestyle. Baby is going to finish up with their development this trimester, and Mom is likely to get a lot more uncomfortable this trimester. You may see a resurgence of first trimester symptoms, as well as some new ones that come with fluctuating hormone levels and the expansion of Mom's belly. This whole trimester will likely be spent scrutinizing every symptom for signs of labor. Updates get shorter this month as Mom's symptoms get more consistent, and baby finishes cooking up in Mom's oven.

## WEEK 27

*How is Baby?*

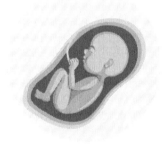

As the baby grows, you might feel some small, odd movements from the baby; as the baby's diaphragm and lungs develop, they start to get the hiccups! They can even get hiccups if Mom has been enjoying spicy meals, since they're not accustomed to those types of foods yet.

The baby is also reaching a point where they may recognize and respond to the sound of voices they hear regularly. Granted, the sound is muffled through their waxy vernix coat and the layers of muscle and tissue of Mom's belly, but by the time they're born, they'll be fully familiar with you and Mom's voice.

*How is Mom?*

This trimester, Mom should be expecting sweat. Between carrying the extra weight of the baby and the mix of hormones at play, she should be staying hydrated, and doing what she can to wick the extra sweat away. With this comes swelling extremities and potentially heat rash. She might also notice that her belly itches even more as it continues to expand; keep moisturizing lotions and oils handy to help relieve the itch without scratching. Here's a little tip for Mom: if you *must* scratch, use your knuckles!

Now that baby is getting a lot bigger, Mom might be finding it hard to keep control of her bladder. Laughing and sneezing are going to be risky if she doesn't want to pee herself, especially if she's staying on top of hydrating properly.

*How Can Dad Help?*

Two areas you can help right now is researching car seats, and getting into an infant CPR course. The safety standards for car seats are updated regularly by manufacturers and governments, so make sure the one you choose is the safest option for your baby and your vehicle. As for CPR; let's be honest, babies aren't great at swallowing in the beginning, and they love putting things into their mouths. Knowing how to handle a choking baby is invaluable in those life-threatening situations.

This is also a great time to be talking to family and friends about making sure their vaccines are up to date. Whooping cough vaccines, for example, don't cover a person for their entire lives, and whooping cough can be lethal for an infant. Anyone who is coming in to visit the baby, especially as a newborn, should make sure they're vaccinated, wash their hands, and don't kiss the baby for any reason. All kinds of viruses can be passed from a kiss to a baby, so play it safe while their immune system develops.

## WEEK 28

*How is Baby?*

By now, baby is settling into their final birthing position. Their development is progressing; they are sticking out their tongue, blinking their eyes now that the lids are no longer fused, and even dreaming! At this point, the baby can experience REM sleep, which is the point in our sleep where we dream, so they may be dreaming about meeting you and Mom!

*How is Mom?*

Now that Mom is in the home stretch, she will be getting even more uncomfortable. Sciatic and lower back pain are on the rise, and in combination with the heat rash and sweating she may be experiencing, she may find that her skin is becoming even more sensitive lately. Breathable fabrics, SPF, and lots of water will help to decrease her discomfort.

*How Can Dad Help?*

If you've chosen a location to birth, it may be a good idea to go down for a tour and get a rundown of what birthing in that location may look like. Reaching the delivery room is going to be a different experience for every couple and every pregnancy, so you're better off knowing where you need to go and what is available to you and Mom, instead of panicking when you arrive.

It's also time to have the circumcision talk if you're having a boy. Some places will no longer automatically provide circumcisions, but if it is a part of your religious or cultural practice, it should be discussed soon.

This is also the point to start counting kicks! There are a variety of apps to choose from to make it easier, and it'll give you an idea of your baby's activity. Try to count at the same time every day, preferably at a time when the baby is usually active. That way, if there's ever any concern about the baby's activity, you have a baseline for activity that you can reference back to and know what is normal for the baby.

## WEEK 29

*How is Baby?*

Baby is focusing on putting on fat, so their wrinkly suit-like skin is filling out with more squish. They may even begin smiling this week, particularly while dreaming. With the baby putting on weight and the womb getting much tighter, their kicks and movements are going to be more prominent, and may be more like a jab than a kick.

*How is Mom?*

Restless leg syndrome usually sets in for a lot of moms during the third trimester. If Mom can keep moving about, it may help to reduce the effects, and let her get some of the rest she desperately needs. Braxton-Hicks contractions can also happen more often, so having a contraction counter can help to recognize when the true contractions have started.

*How Can Dad Help?*

How is the nursery coming along? Mom is getting more uncomfortable, so getting the nursery decorated and filled in will take a good amount off your plate, in terms of planning for baby's arrival.

If you and Mom have been interested in banking cord blood, now is the time to ask your doctor about the process. Cord blood can be an incredible resource, and more parents are considering the painless procedure: whether to have it banked or donated. Discuss with Mom if it's something that you may want to have done.

## WEEK 30

*How is Baby?*

Baby is putting all of their energy into developing their brain right now. Little wrinkles are developing over the surface of their brain, making room for new brain cells. They're also developing their grip strength, so in future ultrasounds, you may see the baby grabbing their feet or playing with the umbilical cord, which serves as their only toy in the womb. Now that the baby is putting on fat, the lanugo is starting to shed, so baby likely won't be super furry on their way out into the world.

*How is Mom?*

Some of the less comfortable pregnancy symptoms of the first trimester may be making a return at this point. The biggest one is typically heartburn; that baby has strong legs, and they're probably pushing on the stomach pretty firmly. Mom is most likely experiencing fatigue all over again, combined with an aching body, and potentially even returned morning sickness.

*How Can Dad Help?*

Pillows are probably going to be Mom's best friend. Do what you can to keep Mom comfortable, because the next ten weeks aren't going to be super comfortable. If Mom usually likes heels, it may be time to keep some flats in the car for her, just in case the swelling gets to be too much. Speaking of the car, try doing a test drive from your work or home to the hospital, so you know exactly how much time you're working with when labor starts. Remember to add in time for traffic depending what time of day you'll be going.

## WEEK 31

*How is Baby?*

Baby's brain is in overdrive, making new connections within the brain to develop the five senses. They'll be sleeping a lot more while their brain develops, and moving a lot more than before when they're awake.

*How is Mom?*

You can expect a lot of the same in the coming weeks; Mom is short of breath, her back constantly hurts, and pregnancy brain has her looking for the glasses that are sitting on her head.

*How Can Dad Help?*

It's time to get the hospital bag locked and loaded with everything you need, since you never know when labor might start. Start packing the things you'll need as you think about them, and refer to Chapter 8 to get a better idea of things you might need to pick up.

Now that Mom is getting much bigger around the belly, you might be wondering if it's still okay to have sex if she's in the mood. As long as her water isn't broken, she's safe to have sex if she wants to. There are no concerns over whether you might hurt the baby; in some cases, you may even lull the baby to sleep with the rocking motion.

## WEEK 32

*How is Baby?*

With the exception of its lungs, your baby's organs are fully developed. If they were to be born now, they'd be viable, though would still need a little help breathing. They're already breathing in amniotic fluid, but their lungs aren't quite there yet.

*How is Mom?*

If Mom's breasts weren't leaking colostrum before, it may begin to happen soon. This means breast pads are going to help her stay dry, without the giant wet spots down the front of her shirt. Otherwise, her symptoms are likely staying consistent.

*How Can Dad Help?*

Get brushed up on the early labor signs, and be ready! At some point in the next two months you'll need the knowledge to recognize early labor if Mom doesn't pick up on it first.

## WEEKS 33 - 40+

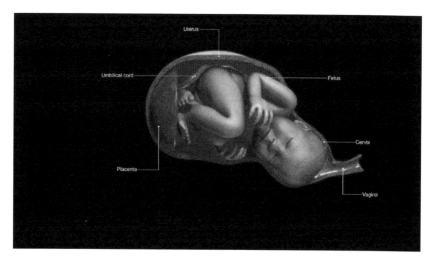

*How is Baby?*

Baby is making strides, and doing any fine tuning it needs. The baby fat has made it so that baby isn't so transparent, and the thinning uterus around them is letting them learn day from night. Their wax coating sloughs off during this period as well, leaving soft baby skin when they're born. More importantly, baby's immune system is finally developed! It's still new, but will continue its development over the next several years. From here on out, baby's development is solely focused on finishing up those lungs and the digestive system, and putting on baby fat.

*How is Mom?*

Insomnia, heartburn, and back pain are Mom's reality right now. Her bladder is going to be in overdrive for the rest of the pregnancy, and she's probably anxious for the baby's eviction date from her uterus. Braxton-Hicks contractions are probably giving her a run for her money, but before you know it, it'll be the real deal! She may also notice some vision changes again, with slight blurring. Her eyes should return to normal after delivery, but for now, she might need reading glasses.

*How Can Dad Help?*

This is the point where all the final details are put into place; getting the car seat secured in the car, making sure that the go-bag is ready, and double-checking everything in the nursery and house for babyproofing and safety. Get familiar with the baby gear you'll be using, so you're not figuring it out with a baby in your arms.

# CHAPTER 8
# GETTING READY FOR BIRTH

 "A new baby is like the beginning of all things – wonder, hope, a dream of possibilities." — Eda LeShan

WHEN YOU'RE in the final weeks and months before the baby arrives, it's time to go over the final checklists to make sure that

everything is ready for the magic moment when the baby decides to make their grand entrance into the world. Everything from getting the baby's areas in the house set up, making sure that all of the essentials are in place, having your hospital go-bag ready, and having one final big outing with your partner before the baby arrives are likely on your mind by this stage. The baby will be here soon! Are you ready?

## ESSENTIALS FOR BABY'S ARRIVAL

If this is the first child between the two of you, figuring out what really is essential and what is a money-grab can be overwhelming. The best thing you can do is to talk to people who have recently had children; someone who had a baby ten plus years ago isn't going to be as keyed in to what is being used today, although they absolutely will have good advice along the way. As someone with multiple children in the last handful of years, this is what I'd recommend as the absolute essentials for your baby, especially in the first year:

- Lots of clothing in a variety of sizes. You won't need an extensive amount of the newborn size unless they're born a premie, or the baby is just very small when they're born. Most babies will grow out of a newborn size very quickly, so focus on having more in the 3-6 month and the 6-9 month sizes. On that note, it's often better to get infant clothing secondhand at consignment and other secondhand marketplaces. They'll grow out of the onesies and outfits you get them in a heartbeat, so save the brand-new purchases for the things that you know you're going to want to keep as a memento, like the first outfit they wore in the hospital, or the outfit you bring them home in. It's a good idea to have a decent amount of clothing for them though, as they'll often go through 2-6 outfits in a day just from spitting up and diaper blowouts alone. Be prepared to do a lot of laundry! I also recommend that if you're getting full body onesies, try to stick with the ones that have a zipper, rather than a whole bunch of buttons. The buttons are cute, but babies are squirmy, and some get sick of getting dressed pretty

quickly. If it's a onesie that just has the three buttons in the diaper area, it's not so bad, as it can be done up quickly.
- On the note of clothing, don't get 20 pairs of shoes for an infant. For one, they can't walk. Second, they don't keep th on. It doesn't hurt to have a pair of booties in a few sizes for transporting them outdoors, especially in the winter months, but getting them shoes to go with every outfit is going to turn into a waste of money very, very quickly.
- Baby grooming sets. The nice thing is, most hospitals will provide things like aspirators, combs, and baby-appropriate nail clippers. Otherwise, keep it simple. You can usually find these kits at your local dollar store. Make sure that any shampoos or soaps that you use are free of strong scents and harsh chemicals for their sensitive skin.
- A variety of bibs. They make them with teethers on them, with scoops to catch food in when baby starts on solids, and in large and small sizes depending on absorbency needs. Once the baby starts teething, it's going to be drool city, so you're going to be changing the bibs quite often.
- Stockpile diapers. Newborn sizes—you can usually get away with only needing one, maybe two packs before they move on to the next size up, but the size one to three, you can't go wrong with having a good pile ahead of time. Newborn diapers are easier to pick up on an as-needed basis, versus having to find a way to get rid of several packages that you now don't need. This applies to cloth diapers as well, if you choose to go that route.
- Sample sizes of diaper creams. There are a few zinc-based diaper creams that some people swear by, but it really does depend on the baby. Test them out for your preference and what works best on your baby's skin, *then* go get the big container of the one that works.
- A diaper genie. You don't necessarily need to go for a specific brand, but definitely get a container that seals well for diapers if you're going the disposable diaper route. Even if you're going for cloth diapers and wipes, you'll want something that

will seal so that the room, and by extension your house, doesn't smell like baby poop and urine constantly. If you're a family that changes the trash daily, dropping any solid waste into the toilet to be flushed, then rolling the diaper up to be tossed in your trash can should also be fine.

- Changing pad. This is a large foam pad with lifted edges and a strap to buckle in your squirmy baby. These are light and portable, so you can keep it where you spend the most time with your baby—and with the waterproof cover on it, you can keep your furniture safe from baby's waste.
- Some toys… but don't go too crazy. More often than not, if people aren't sure what they want to buy for your baby, they'll default to stuffed animals. Try not to go overboard on buying massive amounts of stuffed toys, and instead use the baby toy money on sensory objects, and toys that will help your baby when teething and figuring out how to use their hands. Keep it simple; after all, the baby is going to be in the "just trying to figure out how to be human" stage for a while, so a room packed with toys isn't going to make a difference to them for a while. Small things that fit in their hands but not in their mouths are great, especially if they make little noises and have different textures to experiment with.
- Moses basket. This is going to be a better alternative to a bassinet. It's small, and will make for a safe place for baby to sleep wherever you want them. Even if you put them down in the living room, but want them to sleep in their bedroom, they can be easily transported to the nursery, and the basket placed in the crib. Bassinets aren't used for very long, since they can only be used up to a certain size and weight, so you're better off with a Moses basket and crib combo.
- Crib. On that note, definitely get yourself a crib sooner than later. It's better to get them used to the crib right away, so find something that will fit into your room while the baby shares the room, and that can be comfortably moved into the nursery when it comes time. If a crib won't fit comfortably in your room, a Pack N' Play is a great alternative, since many come

with a lifted piece so that you can more comfortably bend to place and pick up baby.
- Baby monitors. There is a lot of variety on the market, but you don't necessarily have to go for the baby-branded monitors. There are lots of cheaper video and sound monitors that can connect to your phone that you can make sure are on a secure connection. These cameras can typically pick up sound and movement, and lots of them even have sensors to detect a person or a certain sound range so that you can hear the baby cry no matter where you are in the house.
- Baby feeding chair. While high chairs are the norm—and the baby absolutely needs a place to eat—high chairs can be a nightmare for storage and space, and have all kinds of nooks that food can get stuck in. Instead, a seat that attaches to the chairs of your dining set tends to be a lot better overall; they're usually more cost effective, easier to clean, they fit into the average dining room much easier, and they get your baby used to eating at the kitchen table right from the start.
- A stroller that suits your lifestyle. If you know that you're not someone who is a runner or jogger, an expensive jogging stroller likely isn't for you. Choose something that you know will easily come together and collapse when needed, and matches the lifestyle you have.
- A car seat. In the beginning, most car seats are smaller carriers that can be clipped into a base. From there, you'll need something that fits into your car, and has the adjustments for angle and height as your baby grows. Pay attention to things like age conversion seats that will move from rear facing, to forward facing, to booster seat. Also avoid picking up a second-hand car seat from a source you don't know; if a car seat has been in an accident, there may be damaged components that can be dangerous if you were to be in an accident with your infant.

Nice to have but not essential:

- Wipe warmers. While they may seem like a nice luxury to keep your baby warm and comfortable, they can also be a breeding ground for bacteria. Holding the wipe in your hand for a few moments is often enough to warm it up, without risking an infection or rash for your little one.
- Changing table. While they may seem to be the ultimate necessity, the reality is that you're likely going to change your baby wherever it's convenient. It's not so bad if you get a crib that ages with the baby into a toddler bed; some of those types do have an attached changing table that later becomes a part of the child's dresser. Going out and buying a changing table—especially if you know the baby's nursery is upstairs while you spend most of your time downstairs—ends up being a waste of money for many people. A changing pad that can be put down is a far better option if you're looking to save money.
- Bath thermometer. While the marketing for these little gadgets focuses on how sensitive baby's skin is—and of course we want to keep our baby from being burned—we can easily test the temperature with our hands. Lukewarm water is best, so save the money and just use your hands.
- Special "babies only" detergent. While there are plenty that are marketed specifically for babies, along with the "babies only" hefty price tag, what you really need to focus on is making sure that you're getting a detergent that is free of dyes, scents, and other additives. Plenty of all-natural laundry detergents cater to this while offering the cleaning power necessary for the mountains of laundry you're looking at.
- Excessive crib accessories. We love scrolling Instagram and seeing all of the perfectly matched aesthetic crib setups, with the bumpers and stuffed animals and pillows and matching blankets. While this is so cute to look at, it actually creates a hazard to your baby. Minimize what is in the crib so that you can minimize SIDS risk, and keep your baby safe. As the baby grows, having too many

items in the crib also provides your child with a means to climb out of their crib, and may result in injury if they fall.
- Baby tubs. There are plenty of seats on the market that make it easy for baby to be bathed in the sink or tub, and enjoying a bath or shower with your baby is one of the purest bonding moments you can have.
- "Baby Bullet" food processors. If you already have a food processor, it's going to do the exact same thing. There's nothing wrong with choosing to make your own baby food, but you don't need the baby branding that's going to raise the price for something half the size that'll clutter up your counter even more.
- A diaper bag. Even if you don't get one of the traditional branded diaper bags, choosing a favorite tote or backpack is going to do the job. As long as you have the room for the essentials that you'll need, like bottles, snacks, diapers, wipes, creams, and extra clothes in case of a mess.

## HOSPITAL GO-BAG ESSENTIALS

Having a bag ready is key in making sure that nothing essential gets left behind in the rush to get to the hospital. There's never a real way to know that Mom is about to go into labor, unless you have a scheduled induction or c-section. If you don't have one of these scheduled appointments, get your hospital go-bag ready a few weeks in advance, just in case of an early labor. Things that will be necessary or helpful to keep in the go-bag include:

- Important documents. Anything that you may need, whether it's medical insurance, hospital forms that are pre-filled, or identification should be quickly accessible.
- Birth plan. Your birth plan should be kept with your hospital documents so that it is readily accessible to medical professionals. You never know if your usual doctor will be on rotation that night, so make sure that the information is

thorough on the birth plan, on the off-chance that it's a new-to-you doctor delivering your baby.
- Cash. Keep a little bit of cash for vending machines or for use in the hospital cafeteria. It's always a 50/50 chance that the cafeteria in the hospital might use machines, or might be cash only, so better safe than sorry.
- Lip balm. Hospitals are very dry, so keep some lip balm or a chapstick on hand.
- Sugar-free hard candies or lozenges. Keep these sugar-free, since sugary candies can actually make Mom more thirsty. During active labor, Mom's water intake will be limited. This is for multiple reasons; if mom gets an epidural, getting up to go to the bathroom won't be possible, and when it comes time to start pushing, access to the urethra to empty the bladder may be difficult. While mom may be able to have a catheter for a while, depending on how labor is moving, if they have to regularly remove and reinsert the catheter, there is a chance for infection. If there is any reason that Mom may need to be put under for emergency surgery, keeping the stomach empty of fluids or food also prevents the accidental aspiration of the contents of the stomach into the lungs. The final reason, of course, is it makes a doctor's job more difficult to do when they're dodging a stream of urine to the face.
- Headbands or hair ties. If Mom has long hair, it will help her to tie it back when active labor comes along. Labor can be a sweaty time, so Mom needs to be able to focus on what she's doing, rather than fussing with her hair being stuck to her eyelid or in her mouth.
- Toiletries. Don't forget things like deodorant, toothbrushes, toothpaste, hair brushes, and moisturizers. After the delivery, Mom will also at some point want to take a shower while still in the hospital, so make sure that she has shampoo, conditioner, and soap available to her.
- Towel. At least one good towel will likely be far more comfortable than the hospital towels available. They tend to be

thin, small, and scratchy, so one of Mom's favorite towels will go a long way.
- Robe. Between making it more comfortable to walk to and from the shower, as well as being more comfortable to sit and breastfeed in (if Mom is planning on breastfeeding), a good, comfortable robe will make all the difference.
- Pillows. Much like hospital towels, hospital pillows don't tend to be the most luxurious on the planet. You'll likely spend a few days in the hospital, so make sure that everyone has every little bit of comfort available.
- Sweaters and other comfortable clothing. This is for both Mom and Dad. Hospital temperatures can be unpredictable, so you'll want something that will keep you warm and comfortable, as well as something that gives you the option of keeping cool. Bring something that can easily be opened for Mom, such as a button up flannel or a zip up hoodie; something that will make it easiest for her to be checked over by doctors, or to feed the baby when needed. You should have a few changes of clothing for yourself, Mom, and the baby.
- Nursing pads and maternity bras. Regardless of whether or not Mom plans to breastfeed, nursing pads will help to alleviate the leaking, and the maternity bras will offer support when her breasts engorge with milk following the birth.
- Bottles. If you plan to bottle feed rather than breastfeed, it can be best to bring the bottles that you hope to use so that the baby gets acclimated to them right away. The hospital will have some bottles, and will often have samples of formula for you to choose from, but if you already have formula, it doesn't hurt to bring some along with you so the baby is on a consistent formula.
- Charging cord, laptop, and/or bluetooth speakers. At some point during the stay, you and Mom are going to want some kind of entertainment. Any cords should be extra long, since you never know where you'll find an outlet in the hospital room. The bluetooth speaker will also be helpful if Mom wants soothing music during labor. Having a nice long playlist pre-

made can be helpful, since you never know how long labor is going to last. Headphones also don't hurt to have for when Mom is up late breastfeeding, and wants to catch up on her shows in peace.
- Non-perishable snacks and water bottles. This is both for Dad to sustain himself with during labor, as well as for Mom to snack on between meals. Recovery and breastfeeding takes a lot of energy!
- Adult diapers. While the hospital will supply giant pads and mesh underwear to hold the pad in place, adult diapers tend to offer more comfort and peace of mind that everything will stay in place. Mom is going to be bleeding for a while, so she should be able to stay as comfortable as possible.

## SIGNS OF LABOR

The body preparing to go into labor isn't as simple as tv and movies would have you believe; the water breaking and sending Mom into having contractions isn't actually typical. The signs of labor can actually start weeks ahead of the actual birth, so knowing what to look for can help when Mom is shouting at her belly "Will you come out already?!"

- *The baby drops.* Just when you think Mom's belly can't get any bigger or more pronounced, the baby decides to settle in. The baby shifts lower into Mom's pelvis, getting its head in position above the cervix and into the pelvic bone.
- *Joints start feeling more loose or sore.* The hormone production in Mom's body is shifting towards relaxing the body so that the baby can more easily make its way out of the body. This means that the joints through her body are going to feel sore and loose, especially in the hips, knees, and ankles.
- *Cramping and pain through the lower back.* Mom's muscles are now shifting to get her body into the best position to birth in, which means she'll be feeling some soreness. The cramping might feel similar to menstrual cramps as her spine and hips

begin to get into a slightly different position to accommodate the baby's arrival.

- *Bloody show.* This sounds way more graphic than it actually is. The bloody show comes along with losing the mucus plug—the mucus film that covers the cervix to protect the baby from infection—which begins to separate. This might happen in one big clump, or it might break down into smaller pieces that are hardly visible. In the days before labor begins, the vaginal discharge may become thicker and more pink in appearance.
- *Dilating cervix.* This can begin far before labor is impending; some women spend weeks or even months dilated to 1-3 centimeters. The cervix begins to dilate, opening to allow the baby to find its way into the world. Once labor really begins, the cervix will dilate up to 10 centimeters, allowing the baby to pass through the birth canal.
- *The water breaks.* This is one of the most commonly known signs of labor. This is a natural part of the process, caused by the baby's head putting pressure on the amniotic sac, causing it to rupture. When this happens, Mom might feel a little 'pop' feeling, followed by a trickling of fluid, or sometimes a small gush. It may be helpful to put a pad in place so that the fluid can be collected, and Mom can track her fluid loss. If she's filling many pads in the span of a few hours, labor is definitely incoming!
- *Contractions.* The other best known indication of labor is the arrival of strong, steady contractions. While Mom has likely been experiencing Braxton-Hicks contractions for a while now—which are irregular in timing and can vary in intensity—true labor contractions will often be stronger. The contractions that set in before labor will be evenly spaced, getting closer together as the time for delivery gets nearer. While the intensity of Braxton-Hicks contractions will vary over time, labor contractions will gradually get stronger and more intense.

## THE BIRTH

Expectations for the birth will differ depending on a variety of circumstances. A hospital birth will be a vastly different experience than a birthing center or home birth, and the care provider will also have a big influence on how the birth will proceed. Any health conditions that Mom had prior to the pregnancy, or that she developed during pregnancy, will also alter the expectations that you might have for the birth. When it comes to what to expect, it is best to consult with your medical care provider to cover anything that may occur, as it can be detrimental to Mom's birthing and postpartum recovery to go in with ideas of what the birth will look like without the realistic approach of the person who will be guiding the birthing procedure. Every pregnancy and delivery will likely look different, so expectations should stay open and fluid. Much like the birth plan, the birthing experience is unpredictable, so be ready to go with the flow of progress, and know that unexpected changes may occur, if necessary to the health and wellness of mother and child.

*What Can Dad Do?*

When it comes time for the birth, the best thing that you can do is be there for support, and be an active partner for Mom to rely on. Taking a Lamaze or Bradley Method class can help you to be an active participant in the birth. These classes will provide knowledge on breathing techniques, wellness during pregnancy, and hands-on practice with pain relief techniques. If these classes are not available to you, or if they weren't within your budget, learn about helping Mom to breathe through the pain, and be there as a support to hold her hand, wipe away sweat to keep it out of her eyes, and otherwise help Mom and the birthing care professional with anything they may require assistance with. Learning techniques to apply pressure on the hips and back to relieve the pain can go a long way.

# CHAPTER 9
# THE FOURTH TRIMESTER

 "When they finally place the baby in your arms and you notice that smile, you suddenly feel a surge of overwhelming, unconditional love that you never felt before." —Unknown

THE NEXT PERIOD following the birth of your child is known to many prenatal and postnatal professionals as the "fourth trimester."

This window of time is for Mom's recovery and adjustment to now being a mother. This includes you, too. How you support her is going to make a big difference to how she perceives *her* world, especially while looking through hormone goggles.

## FINDING YOUR ROUTINE

Your entire world is going to revolve around this new baby, as well as taking care of Mom, who is also entirely focused on the baby. I guarantee, there has never been a point in your life where you've been so obsessed with another person's bathroom habits as when you are the one changing diapers and literally watching their digestive system mature by looking at the contents.

It's important that both you and Mom alternate on having time on your own, as well as finding moments for yourselves to still feel like a couple. Little routines like watching a movie, cooking together, or making each other coffee shouldn't go down the drain; this time period is about nurturing bonds. Bonds with each other, bonds with baby, and bonds with your mental health. The window may only be five minutes, but five minutes to stare out a window with a hot coffee can make the difference, if you take the opportunity.

*Feeding Times*

Baby is going to be pretty much constantly eating in the first weeks; roughly every two to three hours, depending on their appetite. If Mom is breastfeeding, you can offer support by burping baby and bringing her water and snacks, as breastfeeding does take a lot out of her. If bottle feeding, alternate on feedings.

*Sleep*

"Sleep when the baby sleeps" is such a load of diaper filler for most families. It's probably some of the most common advice that you'll get as new parents, and for most people, it simply doesn't work that way. Why? Because when baby sleeps, you finally have the time to do the things you need to catch up on, like cleaning bottles, and doing the mountain of laundry this tiny human has somehow managed to create in the span of a day, or cleaning the breast pump, or just taking time to breathe *alone*. You might even catch yourself staring at this tiny creature you and your partner created, and what feels like minutes suddenly becomes a half hour. Before you know it, the baby shrieks awake, and you realize you've missed out on your *you* time until the next nap. If you're lucky, you might catch a nap when the baby is napping, but otherwise, it almost always seems to be that when you finally lay down and decide to try to catch a little bit of shut eye, the baby pops awake demanding comfort, attention, and maybe a diaper change.

**Nighttime Wake-ups**

For the first weeks, months, and sometimes even years, don't expect to be getting your full eight hours of sleep. Every baby is going to get through their nights at a different pace. Most pediatricians will recommend that the baby has their own bed in your room for the first six to twelve months to best prevent sudden infant death syndrome, or SIDS. This bed should be free of bumpers, bedding beyond the mattress cover, pillows, and large blankets and stuffed animals.

If Mom is breastfeeding, a show of solidarity can go a long way in keeping your relationship strong; you getting up to do diaper changes while she gets ready to breastfeed will give her that emotional support, and show baby that Mom isn't the only parent that they have to rely on. If Mom has started pumping, or if you've chosen to formula feed, you and Mom can also alternate nights, whether it's switching each night, or being on a 2-2-3 schedule so you can both alternate sleeping in on weekends. It's important—both for your bond with the baby, as well as for the bond with your partner—that they feel they can rely on you.

### *Bathing*

Unlike adults, babies don't tend to need frequent baths. Every family will be different based on their climate, but in colder climates, baby will only need baths if they've gotten fairly messy with spitting up. If you do choose to do daily baths, minimize soaps that can dry out skin, and give them a good amount of baby lotion.

## SUPPORTING MOM'S RECOVERY

While the baby is absolutely going to take up a large portion of your time, your partner is going to need every ounce of support, encouragement, and validation that you can muster. Consider that she has just gone through a major medical event that took 40 weeks of anticipation and discomfort to get to; this is then followed by pushing out seven pounds of baby from a very sensitive area. For the next six weeks, the tissues of her cervix, uterus, and vagina are going to be healing, so it is incredibly important to understand that vaginal sex is off the table. When she goes to her six-week postpartum checkup, the doctor will let her know if the healing is sufficient to engage in sex again (yes, even if she had a cesarean), but bear in mind that the cocktail of hormones might mean even if she *can* have sex, she may not be mentally ready. The body continues to reset itself over the next year as the uterus shrinks and organs get back into position, and the hormones alone can make it difficult to get into "the mood."

*After a Vaginal Delivery*

Two of the hardest things after a vaginal birth are going to the bathroom, and moving around. The first bowel movement is an absolute horror show, especially if Mom had an episiotomy. If you want to help her, make sure there is always a squeeze bottle of warm water accessible to her so that she can reduce the burning of urine in the broken skin if there was tearing. A sitz bath, which is a small tub that is placed over the toilet seat to be filled with warm water—and often baking soda or salt—is going to make it slightly easier. The first bowel movement is extremely painful for most women after a vaginal birth, thanks to the swelling and sensitivity of the tissues, and the soreness of the muscles from doing all the pushing, combined with any stitches and tearing. Stool softeners are likely to be helpful, but it's going to be painful for at the least the first few bowel movements.

Getting up and sitting down can also be an issue while there are sensitive tissues inflamed and sore. Getting a doughnut pillow to sit on can help, and gives Mom a little boost so she doesn't have so far to go when standing and sitting. For a few weeks, Mom might need a bit of help getting up and down from her seat, and may struggle with getting in and out of the car, since it typically means sitting even lower than you would on the couch (with the exception of lifted vehicles, which present their own sitting and stretching issues).

## After a C-Section

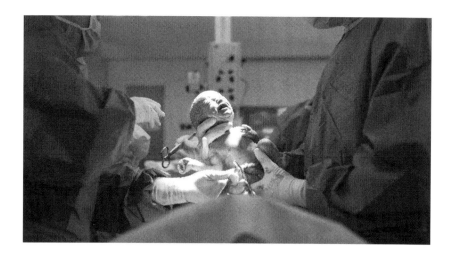

A cesarean is a major abdominal surgery, meaning it's going to take her some time to heal and recover. For the first few weeks, bending down, lifting things heavier than the baby, and general mobility might be difficult for her, so maybe don't ask Mom to bring in the groceries unless it's the bread bag. The body completes its healing from the outside in, so the incision will be healed together long before the incision sites on the organs are completely healed. Even after a cesarean, the body is going to have to reset itself over the next year.

## GOING BACK TO WORK

For many couples, Dad goes back to work pretty soon after the baby's arrival, sometimes days to barely weeks after the baby is born. Depending on where you are and what she does for work, Mom might have six weeks to a year on maternity leave. Going back to work is no easy feat for either parent, after having just welcomed a new child into the world. You worry about the bond you have with your baby suffering while you're gone, and missing the big moments, like your baby's first words or steps. There are a thousand things that will race through your head, like missing your baby while you're at work, and worrying about whether or not your partner is holding up okay while you're out of the house.

*Keeping Your Bond Strong With Your Baby*

After a long day of work, it'd be great to sit back and relax without having to think for a while. Free time is rarely a concept a parent has, and at the baby's young age, bonding is a huge deal. When the baby is a newborn, just getting some snuggle time in and playing tiny sensory games can be great for bonding, as well as letting Mom rest if she's been staying home with the baby. Skin-to-skin contact, baths, and feeding times are great for bonding, and will create memories that you'll grow to cherish as the baby leaves the infant and toddler stages in order to become a whole person on their own.

*Consider Her Perspective; Keep Responsibilities Even*

Don't be that guy who equates 'mother' to 'maid'. Too many guys say "She's at home with the baby all day while I'm out here working; there's no reason she shouldn't be the one handling the cooking and cleaning," or "I'll just do the nighttime wake ups if I'm off the next day so you can sleep in; I need my sleep so I can go to work." You made this baby together—she just did the hard physical labor of forming and birthing your child, and *you are a team.* Yes, you're going to be tired at work, but so is she. It's better to work together and keep a few more ounces of love and sanity than to flush it down the toilet along with your bond and attachment to your partner.

The argument made at these points, especially when the sleep deprivation and frustration sets in, is usually that all she has to do all day is sit around with the baby. This barely scratches the surface of a stay-at-home parent, especially if they're working from home. If she wants to do anything, whether it's work, taking care of herself, or taking care of the home, it's guaranteed she's going to have to do it while carrying the baby, or be interrupted every five minutes to care for the baby's needs. While you're at work, you can focus your time and energy on the work at hand, while also getting breaks where you can eat your own food on your own. You can go to the bathroom without a baby staring you down. You get your commute where you can enjoy silence or your favorite music without interruption. She gets none of that. Parenting is a full-time job that doesn't stop for either of you, and usually comes with none of the healthcare benefits or paychecks.

When you get home, yes, she's going to want to pass the baby to you so she can go enjoy a shower, put on a show, or have time where she gets to take a break and care for herself. It's easy to dismiss that you're out working for bills to be paid, but she deserves credit for the days where she barely gets a moment to feed herself, for the days where she feels she might break down because the baby just won't sleep, and for the work she's putting in to nurture, raise, and care for her baby and the home. Despite how tired you may be when you get home from work, you also have a child that needs time to bond with you, and who needs your care and attention. You may want nothing more than to sit on the couch with your feet up for an hour, but your child does need you, and your partner needs you to step forward for her and your family. Doing things like taking care of bath time and bedtime so that Mom can finally take a moment to rest is being a good partner and parent. Tackling leftover chores together is a great way to make the home feel like it's not falling apart around your ears, and make your partner feel seen and cared for. Alternating nights with the baby not only allows Mom to catch up on desperately-needed sleep, but gives the baby the security of knowing that when they cry, they have two people they can rely on to hold them, not just one.

# CHAPTER 10
# NEW DAD HACKS

> "People who say they sleep like a baby usually don't have one." — Leo J. Burke

## PREGNANCY HACKS

1. **Schedule ahead.** Feel free to schedule all the needed doctor appointments now. That way it's out of the way and you have a clear schedule and plan for the coming nine months.
2. **Every day 'emergency' bag.** Be ready for day to day morning sickness or indigestion while on the go. Fill a small bag, or toiletry bag with things like snacks, ginger candies, peppermint/lavender essential oils, antacid chews. Keep the bag in the car.
3. **Strengthen your bond before the baby arrives.** There will be less time when the baby is born for you and your spouse. The baby will demand most of the attention. Some ways to strengthen the bond include going on regular dates, learning to deal with conflict, and catering to each other's love language. Strengthening the bond will benefit you and the baby.
4. **Use the experience of other new dads.** Join online or in person new dad groups and learn from other new dads.

## NEWBORN HACKS

1. **Bond with baby.** Here are a few bonding activities for dads and newborns. Volunteer for diaper duty and burping duty. Those are excellent bonding times as well as times that mom can get a break. Other ways to bond include skin to skin contact, talking to your baby, and spending as much time with your baby as possible.
2. **Diaper Changing Hack.** One good diaper changing hack is placing a clean diaper underneath the dirty diaper before removing the dirty diaper. That way you can just pull the dirty diaper and clean the baby's bum.
3. **Baby tracker journal or app.** There is a lot to keep track of once baby is born. You need to keep track of feeding, diaper changes, pumping, sleep…

4. **Invest in a good carrier.** A good way to carry baby around and still have our hands free is with a baby carrier. Baby is comforted and we can still get things done… Everyone wins!
5. **Use white noise.** Babies are used to mom's heartbeat, blood whooshing, digestion noises. So a white noise machine provides a familiar environment to fall asleep.
6. **Always have an extra outfit on hand.** Blowouts can happen at any time. Having an extra outfit for those times will be a lifesaver.

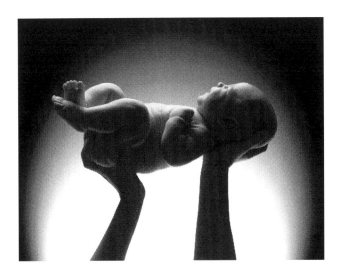

# AFTERWORD

Congratulations, Dad! The next 18 years are going to be a rollercoaster, but they're 100% worth it. For right now, you're looking at some of the most amazing moments with Mom and baby. We're talking first words, first steps, trying out new foods, and most importantly, watching your little baby develop into a person. It's an incredible journey, and one of the most fulfilling aspects of life for those who choose to build a family with their partner.

While lots of attention will be focused on the baby, it's important that you take the time for both you, and your relationship with Mom, as the baby grows and you fall into your new routine.

*Taking Care of Your Mental Health*

Babies are incredibly time consuming. It's important for both you and Mom to be able to take time at least once a week for yourselves; this might mean taking an hour for your hobbies, seeing friends, or finding new ways to meet other parents who understand the journey that you're on. Yes, keeping the house clean is important, but if you're tired, you and Mom can wait to do the dishes or switch the laundry over. Get the rest where you can, even if it's just relaxing in a cuddle puddle on the couch, or curling up in bed for a power nap. Don't fall into believing all the Mommy bloggers who have perfect homes, hair, and makeup who make it seem like the baby has barely changed their lives at all. It's okay to not have it all together, so take the stress off and recognize that as long as the family is cared for, provided for, and has a safe environment, everything is going to be fine. As the baby grows, they'll become more independent, and things like chores will catch up and fall into routine.

*Taking Care of Your Relationship*

Without the relationship, the family doesn't last. At least, not in the traditional sense. In the first weeks or months, you might not find time to go out for a date night with Mom, but it should definitely be on the agenda. Make plans for when baby is a bit beyond the brand-new baby newborn stage, and keep those on the agenda for when you have someone to watch after the baby that you feel safe with. Be prepared that even if you've just decided to go out for supper, both of you will likely be anxiously checking your phones for any distress calls from whomever is watching over the baby. You may even get an hour in, and both of you may realize you're missing your baby. This is completely normal, and just a part of being a new parent.

Even before you manage to get a date outside of the house, don't let romance die. Stolen kisses and compliments can go a long way. Even if you know you're both going to fall asleep on the couch, doing a movie night together every weekend, or even inviting other couples over for food and board games can keep you feeling connected to each other. Romance is in the little things; love notes written on the mirror, caring for each other by getting the other's favorite snack when you're at the store, or supporting hobbies that you have, especially if you have shared hobbies. Taking a hike, going to the beach, or going out for ice cream as a family is a fantastic way to secure the family bond, and keep the romance alive while you're living life with a new baby.

Most importantly for both your mental health, Mom's mental health, and your relationship is to keep the lines of communication open. You have been Mom's biggest support throughout her pregnancy, and the two of you are a team. Don't let yourself think that signs of sadness or anxiety make you a burden. Talk about your feelings, voice your fears and concerns, and be the same kind of listening board for Mom as well. You've both gone through an incredible change, and it's normal to miss your old life, while simultaneously being in love with your new life. It's an adjustment, so take it easy on yourselves, and seek help when it's needed. You've got this! Welcome to life as a father.

---

Please leave a review.

If this book has helped you in any way, please leave a review so that others will find the book as well. Thank you for reading.

Click To Leave Review

*Scan To Leave Review*

# REFERENCES

What to Expect When You're Expecting, 5th edition, Heidi Murkoff.

American College of Obstetricians and Gynecologists, How to Tell When Labor Begins, May 2020.

National Institutes of Health, Eunice Kennedy Shriver National Institute of Child Health and Human Development, When Does Labor Usually Start?, September 2017.

National Institutes of Health, Eunice Kennedy Shriver National Institute of Child Health and Human Development, About Labor and Delivery, September 2017.

Mayo Clinic, Signs of Labor: Know What to Expect, May 2019.

Mayo Clinic, Stages of Labor and Birth: Baby, It's Time!, February 2020.

Kaiser Permanente, The Four Stages of Labor, January 2019.

March of Dimes, Stages of Labor, March 2019.

Wiley Online Library, Journal of Midwifery & Women's Health, Ruptured Membranes: When the Bag of Water Breaks, June 2016.

Babylist. (2021, September 22). *Ultimate hospital bag checklist for mom and baby*. https://www.babylist.com/hello-baby/what-to-pack-in-your-hospital-bag

DiProperzio, L., & Srinivasan, H. (2021, September 24). *9 baby items you don't really need to buy*. Parents.

# REFERENCES

https://www.parents.com/parenting/money/baby-items-you-dont-need/

*Ectopic pregnancy - symptoms and causes*. (2022, March 12). Mayo Clinic. https://www.mayoclinic.org/diseases-conditions/ectopic-pregnancy/symptoms-causes/syc-20372088#:%7E:text=An%20ectopic%20pregnancy%20occurs%20when,is%20called%20a%20tubal%20pregnancy.

*Infertility | reproductive health | CDC*. (n.d.). CDC.

https://www.cdc.gov/reproductivehealth/infertility/index.htm#:%7E:text=What%20is%20infertility%3F,6%20months%20of%20unprotected%20sex.

Marple, K. (n.d.). *Pregnancy week by week*. Baby Center.

https://www.babycenter.com/pregnancy/week-by-week

*Methods of childbirth*. (2004, June 7). WebMD.

https://www.webmd.com/baby/guide/delivery-methods

Mirchandani, A. (2021, October 12). *6 ways dad can prep for pregnancy*. Motherly. https://www.mother.ly/life/dad-prep-for-pregnancy/

*Miscarriage - symptoms and causes*. (2021, October 16). Mayo Clinic. https://www.mayoclinic.org/diseases-conditions/pregnancy-loss-miscarriage/symptoms-causes/syc-20354298#:%7E:text=About%2010%20to%2020%20percent,even%20know%20about%20a%20pregnancy.

Montgomery, N. (n.d.). *Future fathers: 9 ways to help her get pregnant*. Baby Center. https://www.babycenter.com/getting-pregnant/preparing-for-pregnancy/future-fathers-9-ways-to-help-her-get-pregnant_1347929

*Pregnancy week-by-week*. (n.d.). The Bump.

https://www.thebump.com/pregnancy-week-by-week

Reporter, G. S. (2020, June 30). *I started the "gender reveal party" trend. And i regret it*. The Guardian.

https://www.theguardian.com/lifeandstyle/2020/jun/29/jenna-karvunidis-i-started-gender-reveal-party-trend-regret

*What are some common complications of pregnancy?* (2021, April 20). National Institute of Child Health and Human Development.

https://www.nichd.nih.gov/health/topics/pregnancy/conditioninfo/complications

*What health problems can develop during pregnancy?* (2017, January 31). National Institute of Child Health and Human Development.

https://www.nichd.nih.gov/health/topics/preconceptioncare/conditioninfo/health-problems

What to Expect. (n.d.). *Screenings and tests during pregnancy.*

https://www.whattoexpect.com/pregnancy/screenings-and-tests-during-pregnancy/

Brumbaugh DE, Arruda J, Robbins K, Ir D, Santorico SA, Robertson CE, Frank DN. "Mode of Delivery Determines Neonatal Pharyngeal Bacterial Composition and Early Intestinal Colonization." *J Pediatr Gastroenterol Nutr* 2016 Mar 28. [Epub ahead of print] PubMed PMID: 27035381.

Switzerland. World Health Organization. "WHO statement on cesarean section rates." Apr. 2015. http://www.who.int/reproductivehealth/publications/maternal_perinatal_health/cs-statement/en/.

United States. Centers for Disease Control and Prevention. "Pregnancy-Related Deaths." Jan. 12, 2016. http://www.cdc.gov/reproductivehealth/maternalinfanthealth/pregnancy-relatedmortality.htm.

Test Tube Image

United States. U.S. Department of Health and Human Services. Centers for Disease Control and Prevention. Hamilton, B.H., et al. "Births: Final Data for 2014." Dec. 12, 2015. http://www.cdc.gov/nchs/data/nvsr/nvsr64/nvsr64_12.pdf.

# NEW DAD'S FIRST YEAR

EASY PROVEN METHODS TO RAISE A HEALTHY, HAPPY CHILD. INCLUDES MONTH BY MONTH GUIDE AND PRACTICAL BABY CARE TIPS

# FREE BONUSES

**Free Bonus #1   Baby Financial Planning**

In this book, you will learn all about the financial considerations of having a baby.

**Free Bonus #2 10 Activities to Learn Parenting Skills**

In this book, you will get tips on how to build parenting skills even before the baby is born.

**Free Bonus #3 Authentic Connections**

In this book, you will learn new skills to help you nurture your connection with your partner and bring it to a whole new level.

# INTRODUCTION

Remember the day you found out there was a baby on the way? Hard to believe that was less than a year ago. And now, after nine whole months of your partner's pregnancy, the moment has come. You have arrived: a new dad.

Wouldn't it be nice if it were that simple? The reality is, the journey is really just getting started. That might sound intimidating - and it is! But it's only intimidating (and a little scary) because it's the first step in learning more about yourself, your partner, and your little guy or gal than you ever imagined possible. And as you'll find out this year, the first steps always come with some trepidation.

Back in the day, dads were distant figures sort of looming in the background. They tended to be less involved - if not entirely uninvolved - in the birthing process, and often they weren't actively involved in their children's lives. Thankfully, the tide is turning. If you're reading this book, you are part of that change.

More and more research shows that dads who are involved in their child's life have a tremendous impact on their baby's growth, development, and, most importantly - happiness. And what's really amazing is that the flip side also holds true. Being an active participant in your baby's first year is immeasurably fulfilling. There are sleepless nights and challenges, sure - but it's beyond worth it.

But what about those sleepless nights and challenges? That's what this book aims to help you navigate. You'll notice each chapter is divided into eight sections. Here's a little background as to why I chose each category, and what you can expect to learn in each.

**Milestones**

Ah, milestones. I have a love/hate relationship with them. I love them because they're a great way to gauge whether your baby is on track. Let's be honest: every parent, at some point or another, asks this question: "Is my baby *normal*?" And by that, we usually mean: Is he or she doing everything she is *supposed* to do at this age/ stage of development?" This is where milestones are really convenient.

But this is also where the hate part comes in. Because although it's not a bad thing to have standards, the fact is, every baby is different. I know that's kind of a cliche, but as a dad of six, I mean it from the bottom of my heart. Every baby is *truly* different, and milestones should never be taken as dogmatic truths about your baby's development.

If you become concerned about your baby not reaching his or her milestones, be sure to discuss this with your pediatrician. While it's normal for there to be variations in milestone timetables, sometimes dramatic differences might indicate an underlying problem, and often the sooner your doctor can intervene, the better.

**Feeding**

Eating seems like a pretty basic thing, and it is - but it's also the most important thing your baby will learn to do this year. And just because something is natural doesn't mean it's easy!

If your partner has decided to breastfeed, there will be a lot to learn in the first few months, especially, and she will need your support. I've included all my best advice for supporting her in her decision to breastfeed in the following pages.

Not all families decide that breastfeeding is for them, though, and that's okay! There are so many healthy formula alternatives out there to choose from if that is what's best for your family's needs. In this book, you will find advice for bottle feeding your baby, introducing solid food, and when it's time, gradually weaning your baby off the bottle. So we'll cover all the bases, regardless of your family's feeding choices.

**Sleeping**

If you've heard you'll spend the first year of your baby's life as a sleep-deprived dad, rest assured this is only partially true. There are peaks and valleys, and in this book, I've tried to prepare you for some of the sleep challenges your baby (and you and your partner) might face this year.

You'll also find advice for safe sleep, sleep schedules, and sleep training. Because let's face it: while eating might be the most important thing your baby does this year, sleeping is probably at the top of the list for you and your partner.

**Bonding With Baby**

When I first became a dad, I heard a doctor say something that has really stuck with me: "A baby's wants are a baby's needs." This goes for eating, sleeping, and bonding.

Bonding is often thought of as an "extra" need for babies, but nothing could be further from the truth. Physical touch, communication, cuddling - all these things are good for your baby's development as well as your relationship. It's no surprise, then, that you might notice a lot of overlap between bonding and learning. The deeper your bond with your baby, the more he or she will learn from you.

**Learning**

Your baby's brain will double in size during the first year of life, and he or she will experience amazing neurological development. All the physical changes your baby will go through - from learning to eat, to crawling, to walking - are dependent on brain development. As noted by the Urban Child Institute, there are three primary areas of the brain that will grow rapidly during year one, and each area is responsible for specific skills :

1. The Cerebellum: Helps with motor skill development and body control.
2. The Visual Cortex: Responsible for interpretation of visual input and recognition
3. The Limbic Structure: Controls memory and emotion

Although brain development is critical during year one,

learning in the first year doesn't require fancy interactive toys or expensive baby gear. In each of the following chapters, you will find simple ways to encourage your baby's neurological development, as well as build fine and gross motor skills.

**Keeping Baby Safe**

Knowing your home is safe and secure is a key to less stressful parenting. While a lot of these preparations have probably already been made, I've included reminders in each chapter about things to do at each stage of development. You'll also find tips for keeping your baby safe when he or she becomes more mobile - things get really interesting then!

**How is Mom?**

Your partner's body has gone through enormous changes over the last nine months - and now that your baby is here, the changes don't stop! Supporting your partner in the first year is crucial for her health, recovery, and mental well-being. Each chapter has tips for ways to help her take care of herself, from getting back to exercise, to breastfeeding support, to recognizing the signs of postpartum depression.

**How is Dad?**

With all the excitement this first year holds, don't forget to take care of yourself. But that's sometimes easier said than done! During crazy times you might not even know what your own needs are because you're so caught up in being a new dad. I've included monthly ideas for taking care of yourself and balancing work, life, and your own self-care.

A final note: this book does not discuss pregnancy, which is really when all this begins. If you haven't read my book on the first nine months of your partner's pregnancy, check it out!

Overall, here's the takeaway I want you to walk away with as you read this book. When you find yourself overwhelmed by all the demands of the parenting "scene" - because I guarantee, you will - **take a step back.** Get off social media and the internet. Close your eyes and think of the moment you held your baby for the first time. That feeling - that's the heart of it.

I hope this book helps you learn how to change diapers, support your partner, and bond with your baby. But more than anything, I hope it helps you hold onto that feeling. Because that's what this dad thing is all about.

# CHAPTER 1
# BIRTH AND FIRST DAY

WE READ THE BOOKS, took the classes, and did the preparation. As my partner and I walked into our 38-week appointment with our OBGYN, we felt confident and ready for what we were sure would be one of our last appointments before an uncomplicated, natural, vaginal delivery.

There was just one small detail we hadn't anticipated: our baby was breech (head-up instead of the proper head-down position), which meant things would be different from what we expected. After an unsuccessful attempt to turn the baby into a head-down position, my partner went into labor. Within 24 hours of that 38-week appointment, our first baby - a girl - was born.

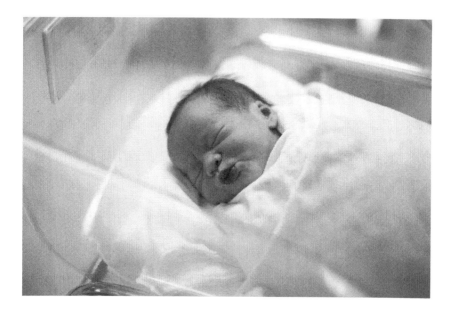

I was totally enamored with my little girl and amazed at my partner's strength. But I couldn't help but also feel overwhelmed. Years later, my memory of the first 24 hours is a total blur.

Looking back, I realize I felt overwhelmed because even though we prepared for what we thought would happen, **we failed to prepare for the unexpected.**

There are a lot of factors that are totally out of your control when it comes to being a new dad. But one thing that you *can* control is how you prepare and the knowledge you obtain before this crazy, life-changing event happens.

With that in mind, here's what you need to know about birth and the first day after your baby is born.

## ROUTINE VAGINAL DELIVERY

### What It Is

"Vaginal delivery" is a pretty big blanket term, and the specific type of vaginal delivery will dramatically affect your first 24 hours post-birth.

Generally speaking, a vaginal delivery is considered "routine" if the following criteria are met:

1. Your partner progresses through the normal stages of labor, with or without pain medication
2. Baby is delivered in a head-down position (in medical jargon, this is called "vertex")
3. Baby takes his or her first breath without any medical intervention aside from a nasal aspirator to clear the lungs
4. The final pushing stage progresses smoothly with minimal stalling and no need for intervention (i.e., forceps or cesarean section).

There are definitely situations when c-sections or operative vaginal deliveries are medically necessary, but in most cases, a routine vaginal delivery is the least complicated way to deliver a baby.

It's totally normal for a routine vaginal delivery to take quite a long time - I'm talking like 24 hours or longer. It's definitely an endurance game!

**What to Expect After Delivery:**

Once your baby is born, your partner will deliver the placenta while the nurses check on baby to make sure all is well and take initial measurements. The placenta is normally "born" within an hour after baby, so if it's taking longer your doctor may administer medicine to speed things along. In the first hour, your baby will also receive newborn tests and any medication you've opted to have administered, such as the vitamin K injection to help with blood clotting and antibiotic eye ointment to prevent eye infections. The doctor will also evaluate your baby's Apgar score (more on that to come).

Then it's time to begin nursing if your partner has chosen to breastfeed. This can be trickier than it sounds! For the first few days, your partner's body produces a substance called colostrum to nourish the baby during the transition into the outside world. Colostrum is packed with all the nutrients the baby needs to adjust. Your partner might feel like she's not providing enough milk, but she is. The baby's stomach is the size of a marble at this point, so it doesn't take much!

Understandably, soreness in the pelvic region is very common in the first 24 hours after vaginal delivery, especially if she experienced any tearing during the process. The hospital should provide pain relief, as well as pads and ice packs to help with that. Your partner might also dread going to the bathroom for the first time - again, understandably! Provide high-fiber snacks to help move things along, and make sure she always has a bottle of water nearby to help her stay hydrated.

## NON-ROUTINE VAGINAL DELIVERY

### What It Is

A lot of people don't realize that a c-section isn't the only kind of operative delivery. Sometimes interventions need to happen during a routine vaginal birth. These are considered "operative" or "assisted" vaginal deliveries. There are two types:

1. Forceps-assisted delivery: This is when doctors use medical equipment called forceps to help ease baby's head out of the birth canal.
2. Vacuum-assisted delivery: Like forceps delivery, during a vacuum-assisted birth the doctor will use a suction cup to draw baby out of the birth canal during the pushing stage.

According to the ACOG, 3 out of every 100 vaginal deliveries will require one of these interventions. So why might this happen?

The most common reason is that the pushing stage of labor has gone on a really long time, and mom just needs help. Pushing is insanely hard work, and when it comes after 24+ hours of painful labor, assistance is sometimes required. The baby might also be in a difficult position, which can make a vaginal delivery more challenging.

Additionally, your baby might not tolerate labor well and show signs of distress, such as heart rate fluctuations, leading the doctors to decide they need to get baby out, stat! An operative delivery shaves a lot of time off of a routine vaginal delivery timeline, which is often in baby's (and mom's) best interest.

**What to Expect After Delivery:**

The first 24 hours after an operative vaginal delivery are similar to routine vaginal delivery. Your partner will be very sore and should rest as much as possible. In the long term, healing can take longer due to perineal tearing, which is much more common during operative deliveries.

An operative vaginal delivery might sound intense, but it's generally considered to be less complicated than a c-section. Just be aware that your partner's recovery will be more challenging than it would be for a routine vaginal delivery.

## C-SECTION

### What It Is

One in three babies in the United States is born via cesarean section or c-section. There are many reasons your baby might need to be delivered via c-section, including failure to progress, fluctuations in heart rate, or fetal positioning. Some conditions your partner may develop during pregnancy might also make a c-section the safest option, such as infections, high blood pressure, and issues with the placenta.

There are two types of c-sections, each of which has its own specific considerations:

1. Emergency c-section: A c-section that takes place as an emergency intervention due to conditions that unfold during the labor process.
2. Scheduled/elective c-section: A c-section that is planned in advance due to conditions that develop during pregnancy. These are typically safer and less complicated than emergency c-sections.

During a c-section, the doctor will administer an epidural and make two incisions: the first through your partner's skin and abdominal wall and the second one into the uterus to deliver the baby. Once the baby is safely delivered, and the placenta has been removed, the doctor will close up the incision site, either with staples, surgical glue, or surgical thread.

**What to Expect After Delivery:**

The first 24 hours after a c-section are a little different from a vaginal delivery. Your partner will be pretty sore in the abdominal area once the epidural wears off, even with pain medicine. Many women find taking their first steps post-cesarean to be very difficult, so reassure her that this is normal and that she has plenty of time to get back on her feet.

Depending on the reasons for the c-section, there may be more interruptions from nurses post-cesarean. This is just to make sure your partner's vitals are good and that there are no problems with the incision, as well as to do routine checks on baby.

In the first 24 hours, it is totally fine for mom to stay in bed as much as possible, although some hospitals might want her to try to walk one time to prevent blood clots in the legs. Most women stay on pain medication for at least a week after a c-section - it is major abdominal surgery, after all! Encourage your partner to rest as much as possible and not rush things.

## IF YOUR BABY WAS BORN PREMATURE

A baby is considered premature if birth occurs before 37 weeks. Since many developmental processes take place during the final three weeks of pregnancy, a premature birth might mean a longer stay in the hospital and a more complicated Day One.

There are three big priorities immediately following a premature birth:

1. **Get Baby Warm:** This is the case for all newborns, but especially for premie babies who can be tiny! They need help thermoregulating and might need to be put on a heating pad or in an incubator to help their body temperature rise.
2. **Establish a Good Breathing Pattern:** The medical team will immediately check baby's heart rate and might need to use suction to help baby clear his or her lungs. Again, this is also common for non-premature babies, especially those with low birth weight, but is more likely if your baby is born early. If baby is struggling to breathe, the medical team might need to use a face mask, breathing tube, or breathing machine to provide some assistance.

**What to Expect After Delivery:**

Depending on how premature your baby is and the circumstances surrounding his or her birth, a NICU stay may be required. The medical team will evaluate your baby's condition and decide on a case-by-case basis.

Keep in mind that if your baby was born at less than 34 weeks gestation, your partner probably won't be able to breastfeed in the first 24 hours. If breastfeeding is important to her, take this time to discuss strategies to build milk supply with the hospital lactation team.

A cool fact: breastmilk that moms make for premie babies has higher protein content and also contains lipase, which helps the baby digest the milk more easily since the digestive system hasn't had as much time to develop.

For the first year of your baby's life - and probably even for the first two years - he or she will probably hit milestones later than the average full-term baby. This is totally normal and no need for concern. Nevertheless, I know firsthand that parents of premies might feel like their baby is "behind." When our son was born four weeks early, I worried that he would never catch up, but eventually he did! Now, nine years later, you would never know he was only four pounds at birth!

One way to ease your mind is to determine your baby's adjust age, right from the start. To do this, start with your child's actual age, or the number of weeks since birth. Then subtract the number of weeks early your baby was. This will give you the adjusted age.

For example, let's say your baby was born three weeks early. His birthday was seven weeks ago. Even though he's been on the other side of the womb for seven weeks, his adjusted age would be four weeks. That's a big difference!

As you read this book, be sure to reference your child's adjusted age to determine what milestones he or she should be reaching at any given time.

## ALL ABOUT APGAR TEST AND SCORES

If you've heard other parents discussing childbirth and delivery, you might have heard them refer to the Apgar test. This is a routine test done right after delivery, in the first minute to be exact. The test is then repeated five minutes later.

| Sign | 2 | 1 | 0 |
|---|---|---|---|
| A (Appearance) | Pink body | Pink body, blue fingers/toes | Pale or blue |
| P (Pulse) | Greater than 100 bpm | Less than 100 bpm | No pulse |
| G (Grimace) | Crying or coughing | Facial change or weak cry | No response |
| A (Activity) | Active, moving | Limited movement | No movement |
| R (Respiration) | Strong cry | Irregular breath | No breathing |

Like any scoring system, Apgar scores are limited, but they do give you a good picture of your baby's health after delivery. Here is a chart that shows the five signs the medical team will look for and what score your baby can receive for each.

Your medical team will add up all the signs to score your baby. For example, if your baby got a 1 for appearance, 2 for pulse, 2 for grimace, 1 for activity, and 2 for respiration, the score would be 8.

Generally speaking, a 5-minute Apgar score of 7 and higher is considered satisfactory. If it's lower than that, the medical team will continue taking the score every five minutes and will administer any medications or other interventions as needed.

Keep in mind that even if your baby's 1-minute Apgar score is low, things can turn around quickly. For example, one of our kids was born with a one-minute Apgar of 6, but by the five-minute mark it was up to 10. He's now six years old, super smart, and definitely not lethargic. Some babies just take a little longer than others to perk up!

## FIRST-TIME DAD TIPS

Regardless of the type of delivery, here is some seasoned dad advice for the first 24 hours post-delivery:

1. **Sleep, Sleep, Sleep!** Your partner will be sore and exhausted in the first 24 hours after delivery. And of course, you'll also be totally wiped out from supporting her and going through the emotional rollercoaster of childbirth. This is why it's great to have the hospital staff change diapers, check on mom, and do other routine tasks. Take advantage of the help and get as much sleep as you can. Now is not the time to learn the ropes - now is the time to get as much R&R as possible.
2. **Connect:** You and your partner have a lot to talk about, especially if things didn't go the way you planned. Additionally, the first 24 hours is great baby bonding time. Babies love skin-to-skin contact, and science says it's one of the best things for them in the first 24 hours post-birth. A study showed that moms who had immediate skin-to-skin contact with their babies experienced lower rates of postpartum depression and that babies cried less and slept more. That's a win-win! It also has been shown to help premature babies adjust and breastfeed. Dads can definitely do skin-to-skin, too, with the same benefits for baby and extra bonding for the two of you.

It's not often you hear the best thing for you to do is chill out, binge Netflix, and enjoy quality time with your partner - but that's really the best thing for you to do now! So kick back and relax (with your tiny newborn on your chest).

# CHAPTER 2
# COMING HOME WITH YOUR NEW BABY

THERE ARE a lot of different opinions on the best time to leave the hospital. Some parents are counting down the minutes until they can leave. Others might enjoy the care from medical staff and see it as an extended date night (especially if the hospital food is actually decent!).

Here's what you need to know about when you'll be discharged and how to survive your first few nights at home as a family of three.

## LEAVING THE HOSPITAL

The number of days you will spend in the hospital after childbirth varies. For an uncomplicated delivery, you might spend two days in the hospital. For a more complex delivery such as a c-section, it might take four days or more to come home.

Generally, you can expect to spend two to five days in the hospital after delivery, but it could be longer than that, especially if there were any complications surrounding your baby's delivery.

You might find it more helpful to think of your hospital discharge in terms of milestones rather than a number of days. Specifically, these five things need to happen in order for you to bring baby home:

**1. Baby Is Feeding Well:** Whether your baby is bottle-fed or breast-fed, the hospital staff needs to know that baby is receiving enough nourishment before sending you home. This is why nurses track the number of dirty diapers your baby has. Too few diapers could signal that your baby is not getting enough milk and might need supplementation. Additionally, if mom is struggling to breastfeed, it's best to get things under control before discharge. Most hospitals have lactation consultants on staff who can help with feeding difficulties during your postpartum stay.

**2. Tests and Exams Are Complete:** Your newborn will have to undergo routine tests and examinations before he or she can be sent home from the hospital. Generally, these will be done in the first 24 hours and might include the following:

- Newborn screen: A routine check for genetic and metabolic disorders such as cystic fibrosis, sickle cell anemia, and congenital heart disease
- Hepatitis B vaccine: Normally given in the first 24 hours after birth
- Newborn examination: Routine check for reflexes, weight, and general physical appearance
- Newborn hearing screen: Routine hearing test to detect any hearing problems

Depending on the circumstances of your baby's delivery, other tests and examinations may be required to ensure your baby gets a strong start at home.

**3. Car Seat Has Been Approved:** If your baby was born prematurely, most hospitals in the United States will require a car seat safety test before postpartum hospital discharge. This test takes 90 - 120 minutes and must be completed before your baby can be discharged since it ensures he or she will be safe for the car ride home.

**4. Mom's Recovery Is On Track:** Regardless of how your baby was born, your partner is going through a challenging recovery. Before you can leave the hospital, the staff needs to know her recovery is on track.

If your partner had a cesarean section or experienced heavy bleeding, you might need to spend a few extra days to make sure she's ready to transition out of the hospital.

**5. Paperwork Is Complete:** No important life event is complete without paperwork, and birth is no exception! You'll need to complete several documents, such as the baby's birth certificate application and Social Security paperwork. Some hospitals also have required classes or reading for new parents that you might have to sign off on before discharge.

While your partner and baby are waiting to leave the hospital, if you have not done so yet, take some time to get the house set up for your baby's trip home. Specifically, here are some things you can do to make sure your first night at home is a smooth transition:

- Tidy Up! New moms need to rest and relax as much as possible, and coming home to messes and chaos doesn't encourage this goal. Make sure the house is clean and in order before you go back home. If you don't feel like you have time to do this yourself, hire a cleaning company to do a thorough clean, or as a friend or family member if they might be able to help.
- Prepare the Sleep Space: Make sure the crib is set up with all the bedding in place, as well as a spare set of sheets.
- Stock the Baby Supplies: Have diapers, wipes, burp cloths, receiving blankets, pacifiers, and other baby gear stocked up and in an accessible location - preferable within arm's reach of your partner's bed, or wherever she plans to rest.
- Stock and Clean the Fridge: Make sure the fridge is stocked with healthy foods you and your partner enjoy. If your partner plans to formula feed or pump breastmilk, set aside some space for bottles.
- Clean and Organize Baby Clothes: Make sure you have a few days of onesies, sleepers, and hats clean for the baby. These should also be put within arm's reach of your partner's sleeping space for easy clothes changes.

- Set Up the Bathroom: Keep an eye on the products your partner is using for recovery in the hospital, such as maxi pads, ice packs, and breast pads. Have a care basket ready for her to keep in the bathroom so she has easy access to her personal needs. To go a step beyond, you can also prepare her a basket of things she can do in bed to stay busy during her recovery period.

## GOING HOME

Once your medical team gives the green light, it's discharge time! Here are some things to think about as you plan your first few days home:

**Transportation**: If you're driving home, take some time to familiarize yourself with the pickup location. Get the car seat installed before you head down to the car with your partner and baby so you can easily transition from the hospital to the car.

If you depend on someone else for a ride, be mindful of your hospital discharge timeline. Remember that you'll also need to be escorted to the pickup area, which can take a while - so plan accordingly!

**Food:** You and your partner have both gone through one of the most intense experiences life can throw at you. Make sure you nourish yourselves with healthy foods that you enjoy and are easily prepared. Don't hesitate to reach out to family, friends, and coworkers to see if someone can organize a meal train for you and the family. There are so many websites to easily create weeks of organized meals during this adjustment period - it's very straightforward!

Whether you have a meal train or not, be sure to have a lot of tasty foods on hand. It can be difficult to go to the bathroom after delivery, so high-fiber foods are a great choice. If your partner seems to be craving high-calorie and high-carb food options, this is totally normal.

Provide a variety of foods your partner likes that will get her metabolism going and give her the energy she needs to adjust. Finally, make sure she stays hydrated - a good rule is to always make sure she is drinking water if she's feeding the baby.

**Healing:** Make sure the environment at home is restful and peaceful. Your partner may be more sensitive to sounds and lighting than usual, which is totally normal. Additionally, it's best to assume mom is not doing any chores for a while. If you need to return to work right away, try to reach out to family and friends in the area to arrange help in the first few weeks, so your partner can focus on resting and bonding with the baby.

**Visitors:** If you live close to family and friends, you'll probably have people ask if they can visit. Be fearless about saying "no" if you think visitors might hinder the healing process, especially during the first few days at home. Some parents find it helpful to have a list of helpful tasks to give visitors when they come over - for example, asking for help doing a load of dishes or folding a load of laundry. Don't be afraid to ask for assistance!

**Communication:** Your partner is processing a lot, and she needs support and encouragement. Understand she might seem despondent or negative, and realize this is a normal hormonal transition. Try not to be critical, which will only make her feel alienated.

If you notice signs of postpartum depression, such as mood swings, lack of bonding between your partner and the baby, irrational fears, extreme fatigue, or anything that suggests your partner is having thoughts about self-harm, reach out to a medical professional.

A final note: it's normal for new babies to sleep peacefully in the hospital, only to wake every hour or two once they get home. This is a very common experience, so plan to take turns rocking and walking with your baby throughout the night. If possible, ask a family member, friend, or postpartum doula to help with these first few nights, to allow you and your partner to get some much-needed rest.

## YOUR BABY'S BIG 3: FEEDING, CRYING, AND SLEEPING

As excited as you might be to come home from the hospital, you may also have an urgent question: what do I do now? Or more importantly, what should I expect baby to do now that he or she is home?

There are three answers. Your baby will:

1. Eat
2. Cry
3. Sleep

Here's how to meet your newborn's three most fundamental needs.

**Feeding**

**Breastfeeding**

Aside from resting and healing, your partner's #1 priority in the first days and weeks postpartum will be to establish a healthy breastfeeding pattern.

That might sound easy, but breastfeeding can actually be a little challenging, especially for first-time moms. Here are some tips to help you help her:

1. **Timing**: Don't worry about a feeding schedule at this point. For the first few weeks, nursing on demand is the best way to establish a healthy milk supply. But naturally, that can be quite demanding! Your partner might feel like she is nursing around the clock. Reassure her that this is normal and will ultimately help her body regulate and provide enough milk for the baby.

2. **Conversation:** Postpartum can be a lonely time, and if your partner is at high risk for postpartum depression, simply taking the time to talk to her while she nurses your baby can be a huge help. Ask how she's doing and what she's feeling. Make it a point to sit down with

her from time to time, just because. It won't go unnoticed and will help her look forward to feeding sessions!

**3. Rest:** Some new moms have a hard time accepting that they need to rest. If your partner insists on being up and about, encourage her to take frequent breaks. This will allow her to get adequate rest and prevent breastfeeding-associated problems like mastitis.

If you notice your partner struggling with any of the following symptoms, encourage her to discuss them with her doctor or a lactation consultant right away, as they can indicate or lead to a breast infection, or mastitis:

- Bleeding or cracked nipples
- Pain during letdown (when her body releases milk to the baby)
- Swelling or tenderness
- Fever

**Bottle feeding**

There are a lot of reasons women choose to bottle-feed, including medical concerns, convenience, or job pressures. Just like the decision to breastfeed, your partner needs to know you are on board and support this decision.

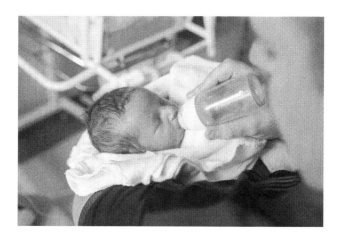

You might hear people say you can't bond with your baby if you bottle feed. Evidence suggests this is *not* the case. Additionally, bottle feeding provides a great opportunity for dads to bond with their newborns.

Here are step-by-step instructions to feed your baby a bottle:

**1. Prepare your space:** Set out a burp cloth, blanket, and anything you might want for yourself at the location you will feed your baby. It's annoying to sit down to feed a newborn and realize you have to get right back up and get something you forgot.

**2. Prepare baby:** Make sure baby has a clean diaper and is dressed comfortably so he's not fussy during your feeding. If your baby likes being swaddled, this would be a good time to get him all swaddled and cozy (better chances he'll take a snooze that way!).

**3. Prepare the bottle:** Wash your hands thoroughly, then mix the formula according to the directions on the packaging. Contrary to popular belief, you really don't *have* to warm baby bottles, although your baby might prefer milk that is warm to cold milk straight from the fridge. If you want to warm the milk, you can run the bottle under hot water for a minute or two. Always test the formula on your wrist to make sure it's not too hot. Avoid using the microwave to heat milk, since it can scald the milk.

**4. Position baby:** This takes some practice, but generally speaking, babies love to be held in a cradle hold position while drinking from a bottle - similar to the breastfeeding position, but slightly more upright. Make sure to support his head and neck. If your baby is prone to dribbling or spitting up, lie a bib under his chin to catch any milk.

**5. Get a good latch:** Once you have baby settled, take the bottle and tap or rub the nipple lightly on his bottom lip until he opens his mouth. You can also just put the bottle in his mouth, but you'll get a better latch if you encourage him to go for it on his own. The baby's lips should be flared and open around the wide base of the nipple, not just the skinny top part.

**6. Position the bottle:** Once baby gets a good latch, keep the bottle horizontal at a slight angle. Make sure the milk completely covers the outlet of the nipple, since baby can get gassy if he inhales air.

At this age, babies usually don't take too many breaks when they're eating, but if your baby seems to be overwhelmed, don't hesitate to take a break and burp him for a minute or two before trying to continue.

It's also very normal for babies to fall asleep while taking a bottle. This generally isn't a problem, but if your baby isn't meeting weight gain recommendations, you might need to stimulate him a bit more during feedings to encourage him to finish his bottle. For example, instead of changing the baby's diaper before a feeding, try interrupting the feeding with a diaper change when he starts to nod off.

### How to Burp a Baby

Once your baby is done with a feeding, it's important to burp the baby. This prevents gas from building up in your baby's tummy, which can cause abdominal cramping and discomfort. There are a lot of different ways to burp your baby, but these are my favorite positions:

1. **The Classic**: Hold baby upright with his head on your shoulder. Gently thump his back to release air bubbles.
2. **Sit-up Style**: This position is best when your baby has a bit of head control. Sit baby up on your knee and pat his back in this position.
3. **Netflix Style:** The classic position to use while you're watching your favorite show. Place baby tummy down across your knees, making sure his head is to the side, then burp away.

Regardless of the position, make sure you have a burp cloth in place in case baby spits up, which is pretty common at this age! When you burp the baby, don't pat her back in the same position the whole time. I like to alternate between patting, rubbing in circles, and rubbing up and down her back to get the air moving.

**Supplements**

For the most part, breastmilk or baby formula provide all the calories and nutrients your baby needs. However, there are a few supplements doctors recommend for the first month of your baby's life:

**Vitamin D:** If your baby is exclusively or partially breastfed, most pediatricians recommend supplementing vitamin D. This important vitamin helps baby develop a robust immune system and prevents rickets. Formula is often fortified with vitamin D, but breastmilk does not contain very much. The other natural source of vitamin D is direct sunlight, which doctors recommend limiting for newborns, so supplements can help make up for any deficiencies. The drops are easy to add to a bottle or some expressed breastmilk.

**Iron:** Usually babies don't need iron supplementation until they are a bit older, but if your baby was premature or born with low birth weight, your pediatrician might recommend an iron supplement.

Aside from these supplements, you probably won't have to supplement your baby's diet of breastmilk and formula. Water and juice are too hard on the baby's stomach at this stage of development.

**Reading Your Baby's Cry**

Crying is your baby's sole means of communication, and while it might seem like crying is crying, that's not actually the case. If you listen carefully, you can hear different types of cries, and each one communicates something different.

Through the years, child development experts have worked out a way to decode a baby's cry. One theory, put forth by a woman named Priscilla Dunston, suggests that babies all make similar sounds right *before* they start crying. Those sounds are:

| Sound | Translation |
|---|---|
| "Neh" | I need food! |
| "Eh" | I need help releasing gas (burping!) |
| "Eaaarrrgh" | I need to poop! |
| "Heh" | I'm too warm/too cold! |
| "Owh" | I need sleep! |

Listening for these sounds is a good way to give your baby what he or she needs before the crying begins. But if you've missed that window of opportunity, there are also many theories about the different cries babies have in the first months of life. For example, some cries just sound like complaining, whereas others sound like your baby is in pain.

A Google search for "how many kinds of cries do babies have" returns some confusing and even conflicting results. I find it easiest to break newborn cries into 4 categories:

1. **Crying from hunger:** This cry sounds angry and growl-like (seriously!). Just like with the different kinds of sounds before crying, it might start with a "n" sound. Child development experts suggest this is because when newborns nurse, the tongue comes in contact with the roof of the mouth, and this cry mimics that physiological response. Whatever the scientific reason, this cry sounds like "I'm angry you're

not feeding me – feed me now!" The obvious response: get the bottle ASAP (or find mom!).

2. **Crying from gas:** This is an unmistakeable, high-pitched scream/cry. It might come in spurts, as opposed to the hunger cries which are more long-winded. You might also notice the baby's face becoming red or that the baby is scrunching up his or her legs. That's a classic gas-relieving posture, and indicates your little guy or gal is having some serious gas. You can help by burping your baby, pumping his or her legs to relieve cramping, or just walking while patting the baby's back and "shushing", which is a soothing sound for newborns.

3. **Crying from discomfort:** This cry is similar to the grumpy hunger cry. If baby doesn't seem hungry or gassy, the crying could be discomfort related to body temperature or a dirty diaper. Start by checking the diaper and seeing if baby needs a change (more on how to do that in a bit!), then feel his or her fingers, ears, and toes to see if you need to swaddle or put on socks or a hat. Or if baby seems too warm, a little skin-to-skin on dad's chest is just the fix!

4. **Crying from exhaustion**: Your baby might just need a nap. If you've had a lot of people over to visit, or recently taken a trip out of the house, he or she could be overstimulated. Go to a quiet room, dim the lights, and walk with the baby while "shushing" and rocking in a rhythmic motion. Again, if you can do this with baby skin-to-skin, even better!

So how much do newborns cry, anyways? I hate to be the bearer of bad news, but they usually cry a lot. In the first six weeks, it's totally normal for a baby to cry got two or three hours per day. Some of that crying is simple to fix, and some of it is unexplained. If your baby has colic, it's normal for him or her to cry 3+ hours.

The most important thing to remember is that at this age, it's best to respond to a crying baby. You might hear some people say picking up a crying newborn will "spoil" him or her, but nothing could be further from the truth. Responding to your baby's cry promptly and taking the time to figure out what's wrong is one of the first ways you establish trust. Put simply, a newborn crying is *not* the same as a toddler throwing a tantrum. So if your immediate instinct is to provide assistance, trust that intuition.

On the other hand, if your immediate instinct is *not* to provide assistance because you're absolutely exhausted, that's also normal! Having a plan in place to take shifts with your partner is crucial here. If your baby has colic, asking a family member for help or hiring a postpartum doula can also be a tremendous help.

Finally, remember this stage doesn't last forever. Your baby is going through huge changes right now, but once things regulate, it gets better. I promise!

**Helping Your Baby Sleep**

Sleep Training and Schedules

Sleep training and schedules are lifesavers…when your baby is older. For the newborn stage, it's best to try to sleep when baby sleeps as much as you can. Most newborns are only awake for 7-10 hours per day, so that's not a bad deal!

It's totally normal for your newborn to have his or her days and nights mixed up, especially in the first week after you come home from the hospital. The best way to cope with this is to simply clear your schedule as much as possible and plan for a week of downtime. The more you can go with the baby's flow, the more rest you'll get.

The bottom line: for now, skip the schedules.

The "Family Bed"

Along with politics and religion, the subject "baby sleeping arrangements" belongs on the list of things *not* to discuss at holiday gatherings.

Before I had kids, I swore I would *never* have a family bed situation. Not only was I raised to believe it was dangerous, but it also seemed like a total invasion of privacy. But as with many things to do with parenting, I've become a bit less dogmatic through the years. And I'm not

alone: a study showed that parents in the United States increasingly report that they have a family bed situation during the first three months postpartum.

Now if someone asks me about my perspective on the family bed, my answer is: it depends.

More specifically, there are two important factors to consider if you're trying to figure out whether a family bed option is for you:

1. **Safety**: Just like a non-family bed situation, safety is of utmost importance if you decide to co-sleep. Here are some non-negotiables for bed sharing:

- Never sleep with your baby on a couch, sofa, or armchair. The safest place is a king-size bed to give baby plenty of space.
- Don't surround your baby with pillows, sheets, blankets, stuffed animals, or any other objects that might be able to accidentally cover his or her face. My partner and I co-slept with two of our babies who had a hard time sleeping separately. During this time, we slept on either side of baby in a king-sized bed. We both used separate bedding (twin sheets and a light blanket), and just a small pillow. This way, baby had plenty of space to sleep in the middle of the bed.
- Never co-sleep with your baby if you have had any kind of medication that affects sleep, alcohol, or cigarettes. It's not worth it the risk. If mom is still taking painkillers from delivery, it's best for the baby to sleep in a separate space to avoid the risk of suffocation.
- If your baby was born premature or weighs less than 5.5 lb, experts recommend you skip the family bed until baby is older.
- Always place baby on his or her back to sleep. Research shows that at this stage, sleeping in a supine position greatly reduces the chances of SIDS.

2. **Sanity**: If bed-sharing causes sleepless nights and stress dreams, don't do it! Likewise, if you and mom sleep better with your baby close by, the added hours of sleep (and therefore parental sanity) might be worth it, as long as all the safety precautions are in place.

If the idea of a family bed isn't quite up your alley, consider room-sharing. Room-sharing is sleeping with your baby in the same room, with a co-sleeper crib or bassinet set up right next to your bed. It's almost like your baby's in bed with you.

This is my personal preference because it provides the advantages of the family bed (helps baby regulate, encourages breastfeeding, and is just more convenient), but allows me to sleep more at ease and not worry about whether I'm going to roll too close to baby, throw my blanket over him, etc.

Finally, perhaps the most important factor is communicating with your partner. Whatever sleeping arrangement you choose, it's important for you both to be on the same page. That might involve some give-and-take on both sides, but it's definitely best to make the decision together.

## SIDS

SIDS (sudden infant death syndrome) is defined as an infant death that occurs in a previously healthy infant, for unknown reasons, during the sleep cycle. I know people personally who have gone through this, and it's a scary thing to think about as a new dad.

There are still so many things we don't know about SIDS, but research has shown a correlation between three risk factors (known as the Triple Risk Model) and SIDS occurrence:

1. Infant vulnerability

2. Baby's period of development (the most critical stage is defined as 2-4 months of age) 3. Environmental stressors (soft bedding, cigarette smoking during pregnancy, unsafe co-sleeping, etc.)

Some exciting research released in 2022 suggested that babies with decreased amounts of an enzyme called butyrylcholinesterase might be at higher risk for SIDS, but the exact causes remain unknown. Until we know more, following safe sleep recommendations, especially with vulnerable infants and those between 2-4 months of age, is the best way to prevent SIDS.

Additionally, the American Academy of Pediatrics recommends sleeping in the same room as your baby for at least the first six months of life. Room sharing allows your baby to regulate his or her sleep by tuning into you and your partner's breathing patterns. Pretty amazing! And of course, that works both ways. You'll be able to keep a watchful eye on the baby if he or she is close to your bed.

Remember, everyone's getting the hang of things in these first few days, so don't get discouraged! Think of this time as the "getting to know you" period. As the days go on you'll start to get a sense for your baby's preferences, which hopefully means more sleep for you and your partner.

# CHAPTER 3
# BABY CARE 101

SO YOU'VE MADE it home and are adjusting to a good eating and sleeping rhythm. Now it's time to level up!

Newborns are actually pretty low maintenance in the first weeks. They might go through a challenging adjustment period when you first arrive home, but once things settle down, they basically just sleep, eat, and poop.

But still, it's a huge change for most couples, and you might feel a little in over your head. Here are some tips for six of the most fundamental baby care needs to help you get your footing:

1. Swaddling
2. Changing diapers
3. Holding the baby
4. Bathing
5. Clothing
6. Basic healthcare

## SWADDLING

Along with "side/stomach", "shush", "swing", and "suck", "swaddle" is one of the famous "5 S's" of infant care put forth by Dr. Harvey Karp, author of the bestselling book *Happiest Baby on the Block*. Why does swaddling have such a mesmerizing effect on babies?

Well, if you think about the way your baby has spent the first nine months of his or her existence - hanging out in mom's womb, in a constricted, warm, comforting environment - it makes a lot of sense! Swaddling simply mimics the baby's initial, familiar environment.

Swaddling your baby may seem daunting, but it's really simple. Nevertheless, I highly recommend practicing with a baby doll the first few times to get the hang of it.

**Swaddling Your Baby Step-by-Step**

1. Fold a swaddling blanket in half so that it forms a triangle (corner to corner), and place it on a soft, open surface like your bed.
2. Lie baby right in the middle.
3. Fold the top right (or left, it doesn't really matter) corner down across the baby's right shoulder and left hip/upper thigh. Tuck it behind baby. You'll have a little bit remaining at the bottom - that's fine.
4. Tuck the little bit remaining at the bottom under the baby's left shoulder.
5. Repeat step 3 with the other side.
6. Tuck any remaining blanket in at baby's chest.

It's that simple! From here, simply pick your baby up and do some of those other 5 S's for ultimate soothing superpowers.

You might wonder whether swaddling is safe for your newborn. A 2014 study in the *Journal of Pediatrics* investigated several cases of SIDS to try to answer that question. According to the research team, instances of SIDS did not seem to be related to swaddling but rather to unsafe sleep conditions (such as baby sleeping on his tummy instead of his back) and items such as bumpers and soft bedding. So rest assured, swaddling is safe and effective.

## CHANGING DIAPERS

Ah, diapers: commonly known as the bane of every dad's existence. But it doesn't have to be this way! Changing diapers is a simple process as long as you have a strategy.

Before you do the deed, you'll need to prepare your space. This means putting some kind of non-precious surface (often a disposable changing pad, but it could also be a paper towel or clean towel) under your baby *before* you begin the diaper-changing process. Additionally, have plenty of wipes (5+ for poopy diapers or 2+ for wet diapers), as well as a few extra diapers close by. Finally, if you're dealing with any kind of baby diaper rash, have your diaper cream of choice open and ready nearby.

Here's a step-by-step breakdown to help you conquer the ultimate dad task. The first few times might be a little slow, but eventually, you'll pick up speed, especially with a properly prepared space. This is important because the longer the process takes, the more likely you are to 1.) upset your adorable baby and 2.) have to change your shirt.

**Changing Your Baby Step-by-Step:**

1. Lie baby down on your changing table or another surface.
2. Undress the baby down to the diaper.
3. Place the clean diaper under the diaper you are about to change. This is important because there's a very good chance

your baby will eliminate pee or poop as soon as you open that diaper. Be prepared!
4. Unfasten the dirty diaper and pull the front down toward the baby's feet while gently bending his legs and bringing his feet up toward the belly. This is your first peek at what's in that diaper. Grab wipes accordingly.
5. Gently clean your baby's diaper area. For girls, be sure to wipe from front to back to avoid infection. There are a lot of crevices down there, so be careful to clean thoroughly! When you've finished, remove the old diaper from under your baby.
6. Quickly inspect the diaper area for any rashes or irritation. If your baby is developing a rash, it's important to wait a little while and allow the skin to dry. I know it seems like an eternity, but it will help prevent the rash from worsening.
7. Apply the diaper cream of your choice once the skin is dry, and gently clean the umbilical cord with a clean baby wipe.
8. Put the new diaper on. If your baby's umbilical stump hasn't fallen off, you can just fold the top of the diaper down so the belly button has room to breathe.
9. Tidy up. This step is the icing on the cake because it's where you will really impress your partner. Don't get me wrong - it's impressive enough that you're changing diapers to begin with. But by throwing any dirty clothes in the laundry and making sure to put the diaper in the appropriate disposal bin, you'll go a step beyond.

That's a wrap. Your baby might be pretty angry at this point - totally normal. Redress the baby and take a little walk to calm him down.

**FAQs About Diaper Changes**

1. **How many diapers per day?** Your baby will have 10 - 12 dirty (wet or poopy) diapers per day. Yes, this means every two hours, on average. Additionally, your baby might pee or poop

at unexpected moments. Yes, that might be when you remove the previous diaper and are most vulnerable. Accepting this fact will allow you to be calm and collected when it happens.

2. **What causes diaper rashes?** There are a few things that can cause diaper rashes. In the first week after birth, your baby's skin might just be extra sensitive. A lot of new babies develop minor rashes that resolve as they adjust.

3. **Do I need diaper cream?** It's helpful to have a few diaper creams on hand just in case your baby develops a rash. However, there are a few other ways you can prevent rashes before they become a problem. The first is to change your baby regularly. Poopy diapers should be changed as soon as possible to avoid irritating the skin. Keeping your baby's bottom clean and dry is key. Second, as scary as it sounds, giving your baby's bottom some air time after each change will also go a long way in preventing rashes.

4. **What kind of diaper cream is best?** This is a hotly debated issue, but the answer really depends on your baby's skin and the cause of the diaper rash. Generally speaking, diaper creams that contain zinc oxide will do a great job of clearing up an already-existing rash. But if you're looking for prevention rather than treatment, all you really need is a barrier to keep your baby's bum from getting too moist and developing a rash. These products are often called "ointments," "balms" or "healing creams."

5. **When should I worry about a diaper rash?** A diaper rash that causes open sores, extreme discomfort, or prolonged symptoms warrants a trip to the doctor. Your doctor may be able to prescribe a stronger cream to clear up the rash.

6. **What kind of diapers and wipes should I buy?** There are so many diapers and wipes on the market, so selecting the one you want to use can be overwhelming. Our kids have done best with unscented wipes and diapers that are designed for babies with sensitive skin, especially during the newborn period. But, like so many other parenting decisions, trial and error is the best teacher here.

7. **What about cloth diapers?** Cloth diapering has become much more popular and manageable in recent years. Gone are the days of giant diaper pins and boiling diapers to sanitize them. Today's cloth diapers are designed to be convenient and cute. That said, it's still quite the undertaking. We cloth-diapered three of our kids but waited until we got the hang of it to start right away. If you plan to use cloth diapers, it can be a little less stressful to have disposables on hand, just in case you aren't quite ready to jump into it immediately.

## HOLDING YOUR BABY

It's amazing how intimidating holding a newborn can be. But study after study shows that babies who are held - ideally skin-to-skin - adjust better to life outside the womb.

I remember being slightly terrified to hold our first baby. She was so tiny and looked like a breakable baby doll. Plus, she was covered in vernix (that white waxy stuff a lot of newborns are born with), which kind of freaked me out. Of course, eventually I conquered my fear and also realized newborns aren't nearly as fragile as they appear.

What's the best way to pick up your newborn? It's hard to give step-by-step instructions, since you're always picking up or being handed the baby at different angles. Let's go through the classic 4 W's and 1 H ("Where, What, When, Why, How?") to touch on some important points to keep in mind when you hold your little one.

**Where:** Your baby feels most stable when you support their most wobbly points: namely, their head (and neck) and legs.

**What:** Keep in mind what holding is, especially in this first month: an imitation of the mother's womb. Based on that image, it makes sense why making shushing noises and rocking the baby would help soothe him.

**When:** Clue into your baby's cues to determine if now is the time to be held or do something else (feeding, diaper change, etc.). I remember feeling personally offended when my baby didn't want to be held, only to later realize it was because I hadn't really taken the time to check in with my partner about the last time the baby had eaten or been changed.

**Why:** Being held is, first and foremost, an act of bonding. It's easy to forget when kids are newborns, but try to remember that those hours you spend holding your baby are establishing a relationship of trust --- *for life.*

**How:** Be relaxed. Babies can be oddly intimidating, but if you take a deep breath (inhale and exhale) before picking your baby up, you're less likely to tense up and make your baby feel squished or stressed. Dads have been holding babies since the dawn of humanity - you've got this!

And don't forget the amazing benefits of holding your baby skin-to-skin. For example, a study found that newborns who were born via c-section and were held skin-to-skin (by dad) cried significantly less than those who were placed in a cot. The babies who received skin-to-skin contact with dad and were held on his chest cried for an average of 60 minutes after delivery. Babies who were placed in a cot cried for an average of 110 minutes - almost twice as long!

The research team concluded: "The infants in the skin-to-skin group were comforted; that is, they stopped crying, became calmer, and reached a drowsy state earlier than the infants in the cot group."

It's totally normal for your newborn not to like being held in any position that vaguely resembles their nursing position, including the popular cradle hold. If being cradled isn't your baby's thing, there are a lot of other ways to hold your baby. Here are two of my favorites:

**The Football Hold**: This is a holding position many dads (including myself) love: the football hold. In this hold, you support the baby beneath the chest, neck, and head, as well as the legs, so that baby is head down on his or her tummy across your forearm. His head should be nestled in the crook of your elbow. Holding your baby in this position often relieves gas, which is why it's often considered a great hold for colicky babies.

**Over-the-Shoulder Hold:** This one is exactly what it sounds like - holding baby upright, looking over one of your shoulders. This is a classic holding position that's great for burping your baby. Just make sure you have a burp cloth under the baby. Eventually, your baby will hold his or her

head up in this position, but for now, be sure to provide support for the head and neck, which can be a bit unstable at this age.

## BATHING YOUR BABY

The skin is the body's largest organ, so it makes sense that a lot of newborns go through some major skin changes in the first week or two after birth. It's totally normal for newborns to have baby acne, dry skin, and blemishes. Keeping your baby's skin clean is the best way to prevent these normal occurrences from becoming more serious problems.

**Bathing Your Baby Step-by-Step:**

1. **Gather your supplies:** Grab your baby shampoo, four washcloths, a few diapers, baby wipes, a baby brush, a nail file/emery board, and a towel. Get two of the washcloths slightly wet and apply a squirt of baby shampoo, then rub the fabric together to get a lather. Keep the other two soap-free, but dampen them with room-temperature water.
2. **Prepare the bath water:** Make sure the water is just a bit warmer than room temperature (around 99 degrees Fahrenheit but not hot. Whether you're using a baby bathtub, a regular bath, or a sink, you don't need a lot of water. A couple of inches will do just fine.

3. **Undress baby.** Don't do this before you prepare the water, or your baby might get too cold. If you're worried about your baby pooping in the tub, it's totally fine to keep the diaper on until the very end.
4. **Place baby in the water.** Support her head and neck with one hand, and bottom and legs with the other. Talk to her with a calm voice as you do this to reassure her it's okay and that you're there.
5. **Bathe your baby's body:** With the soapy washcloth, gently clean your baby from the neck all the way to the toes. If you left her diaper on, you can remove it to clean the diaper area.
6. **Wash your baby's head/hair:** Gently wash your baby's head with the second soapy washcloth. Be careful with the soft spot - you really don't have to apply pressure. This is just to remove some of the oils from the baby's head to minimize cradle cap, which is caused by oil buildup on the baby's scalp.
7. **Remove excess soap:** With the third washcloth, wipe off any excess soap on the baby's body, then do the same on the baby's head with the fourth washcloth. (I like to use a separate washcloth to wash and rinse the baby's head to avoid passing any germs from the diaper area.)
8. **Wrap baby in a towel and take her out of the bath.** Gently dry your baby off, then put on a fresh diaper and clothes.
9. **File baby's nails if needed.** Some parents like to use nail clippers, but I prefer a small emery board. They make them in baby sizes, but you can also use a regular one or even a nail file. Gently file baby's nails down - they grow quickly, and since newborns don't have great fine motor skills yet, it's common for them to scratch their faces!

If your partner or someone else can help with bath time, it's nice to have a second pair of hands. If not, there's another way you can do it that's much simpler: a sponge bath. You don't need to do it in the bathtub or other tub - you can just wipe baby down with a clean, wet washcloth (same temperature of water) and a tiny bit of baby soap if desired. Just make sure to have a clean towel underneath the baby, some warm blankets, and plenty of diapers and wipes close by.

## CLOTHING YOUR BABY

Newborns really don't need a lot of clothes. My partner and I have six kids, and through the years we've managed to get this down to a science. Here's a "bare essentials" wardrobe for the first few weeks:

- 5 footed sleepers
- 5 daytime onesies (long or short sleeves, depending on the temperature) • 5 nighttime onesies (long sleeves preferable)
- 3 sleep sacks
- 5 pairs of footed pants
- 7 pairs of socks
- 5 baby hats
- 5 swaddle blankets

Here's a bit of info about each item and why I consider them essential:

**Footed sleepers:** These are great for taking the baby to doctor appointments or other outings. You don't have to worry about socks (although you can certainly still put them on under the sleeper), and they are easy to put on and take off.

**Onesies:** The classic baby clothing item. Onesies are great because the snaps keep them in place. A tip for diaper blowouts: most onesies have shoulders you can open to pull the onesie *down* and off the baby, instead of *up* and over the baby's head. Better to keep the poop contained in baby's bottom half than to risk any head involvement!

**Sleep sacks:** These look kind of like giant baby sleeping bags, which is basically what they are. Sleep sacks are great because they give your baby freedom of motion while sleeping. Our babies have slept well with a long-sleeved onesie underneath.

**Footed pants:** Footed pants are easy to put on your baby and don't require any socks.

**Socks:** I have a love/hate relationship with newborn socks. They definitely seem to make babies more comfortable, but they're also always getting lost. Still, if your baby will sleep better with socks on, it's definitely worth it to have several pairs.

**Hats:** Babies lose a lot of heat through their heads, so having several baby hats is important. Plus, they're really cute.

**Swaddle blankets:** I consider these a wardrobe item because our babies love being swaddled. Some babies don't, but the beauty of swaddle blankets is you can also use them as regular blankets, burp cloths, nursing coverups for your partner, etc. Choose blankets that are made out of muslin or other natural fibers since these tend to be more breathable and won't cause overheating.

Of course, this is only the bare minimum, and hopefully, you're not doing a ton of laundry, so having more clothing on hand certainly won't hurt. But if you're looking to just get the essentials, this wardrobe should have you covered.

## BASIC HEALTHCARE

### Taking Your Baby's Temperature

The American Academy of Pediatrics recommends taking newborn temperatures either rectally (I know, not what you want to read!). Other methods just aren't as accurate. But don't worry, it's really not as horrible as it sounds.

### Taking Baby's Temperature Step-by-Step

1. Prep the thermometer by wiping it clean with rubbing alcohol. Put a bit of petroleum jelly or coconut oil on the end.
2. Lie baby face down on a soft surface or your lap. It's easiest if he is just wearing a diaper, maybe with a blanket over him if

he seems cold. Pat his back and calm him, so he is relaxed, which will make the process much easier!
3. Gently place your non-dominant hand across the baby's lower back while removing one side of his diaper with your other hand. Pull the diaper back and gently place the thermometer end into the rectal opening - about ½ inch is all. Press the thermometer button and hold the thermometer in place. Keep your other hand on the baby's back and talk to him to reassure him everything is okay. Can't blame him for being a little out of sorts!
4. Wait for the beep, then read the thermometer. Put the diaper back on.

That's it! Newborn temperatures should be less than 100.4 degrees Fahrenheit. If your baby has a fever, contact the pediatrician right away.

**Visiting the Pediatrician**

Your newborn will need to go in for several doctor visits in the first year of life, and a lot of them take place during the first month. These visits are usually pretty straightforward. Your doctor will ask about feeding, sleeping, and any concerns you have, and will check the baby's length, weight, and head circumference to start a growth chart.

Your baby will also receive his or her second hepatitis B vaccination in the first month (the first one is usually administered at birth).

Here's a typical list of your baby's pediatrician visits for the first year of life:

- Birth
- 3-5 Days After Birth
- 1 Month
- 2 Months
- 4 Months

- 6 Months
- 9 Months
- 12 Months

As your baby grows, the pediatrician will ask more questions relating to language development and motor skills.

Mastering these six skills (swaddling, changing diapers, holding the baby, clothing the baby, giving baby a bath, and doing basic health care tasks) covers most of the bases. Before you know it, you'll be wearing your baby to work! Okay, maybe not, but mastering the basics is really all you need to focus on right now.

**Common Illnesses and How to Treat Them**

Infants younger than three months should not have over-the-counter medications like Tylenol or Advil without consulting your pediatrician. This can make it hard to know what to do when your baby comes down with a cold or other illness. Here are some simple ways to deal with common health concerns at this age:

- **Fever**: See your pediatrician as soon as possible. Until you can get in, keep baby's temperature down with cool washcloths on the forehead, light clothing, and frequent nursing if you are breastfeeding.
- **Cough**: Use a humidifier for a dry cough, or sit in the bathroom with the hot water on for a few minutes to help loosen chest congestion. Observe your baby and see your pediatrician or urgent care immediately if baby seems like she is struggling to breathe. Keep your baby upright as much as possible.
- **Stuffy Nose**: Use saline nose drops, followed by a nasal aspirator to help clear baby's nose. The NoseFrida is another option a lot of parents love at this age. Again, keeping the baby upright is also helpful.

- **Dry Skin:** Use a fragrance-free moisturizer after bath time. If the air in your house is dry, a humidifier can help here, too.
- **Eye Discharge:** Gently wipe baby's eye from the nose to the outside corner with a piece of clean gauze soaked in warm water.
- **Vomiting:** Focus on keeping baby hydrated. If vomiting continues for more than 24 hours, or if your baby shows signs of dehydration such as crying without tears or cracked lips, consult your pediatrician.
- **Gas:** Try gripe water (only after baby is one month old - be sure to read the label).
- **Cradle Cap:** My favorite remedy for cradle cap is coconut oil. During your baby's bath, gently massage some coconut oil into her scalp (avoid her soft spot!). Then gently brush her head and watch the cradle cap miraculously disappear!

## FINDING CHILDCARE

Now that you are home and adjusting to life with your new baby, you're probably thinking about the next big adjustment on the horizon: going back to work. For parents who both work full-time, that also means looking for the right childcare arrangement for your baby.

Here are some questions to ask yourself as you search for the best childcare solution for your family:

1. Do I need part-time or full-time care?
2. Do I prefer an in-home daycare, a nanny who comes to watch the baby at our house, or a traditional daycare?
3. Do I have any family members or friends who might be interested in providing childcare?
4. What specific hours do I need childcare?
5. What is our monthly budget for childcare?

In addition to answering these questions, ask family and friends for recommendations to start out on your search for childcare. Visit each potential childcare provider in person before making any commitments. Finding a trusted daycare, nanny, or other childcare provider to care for your baby is one of the best ways to make the transition back to the workplace as seamless and stress-free as possible.

# CHAPTER 4
# YOUR BABY'S FIRST MONTH

 "After waiting for long 9 months, I'm finally relaxed and happy to become a proud daddy of a little angel."
—Unknown

THE FIRST MONTH of your baby's life is definitely a rollercoaster, but it's also an amazing and transformative time. I remember telling my partner after our first child was born that I felt the whole experience had pushed me beyond all the limits I thought I had. Not only did I realize I'm actually way more patient and perseverant than I thought, but it also showed me how much love I was capable of giving. You need a lot of love to deal with poopy diapers and sleepless nights.

Hopefully, you have a totally clear calendar and can enjoy these first four weeks. My number one tip: take advantage of the downtime and enjoy transitioning to life as a family of three. Here's what you need to know about your baby, your partner, and dad life this month.

| Your Baby's Milestones: Month 1 | | | |
|---|---|---|---|
| Eating | Sleeping | Motor Skills | Language |
| Eats about 32 ounces per day<br><br>Takes 3-4 ounces per feeding<br><br>Breastfeeds every 2 to 3 hours | Sleeps an average of 14 hours per day<br><br>Sleeps on his or her back | Learns to suckle at the breast of drink from a bottle<br><br>Still has newborn reflexes such as startle, rooting, stepping, and grasping reflex | Basically just grunts and cries |

## FEEDING

If you feel like your newborn eats a lot during the first month of life, you're right. Newborns go through rapid changes, and they need that nutrition to provide support. Here are a few considerations for your baby's feeding needs in the first month outside the womb.

**Bottle Feeding:** Your baby will gradually increase the amount of milk taken each day throughout the first four weeks, and by the end of the first month, she will consume about 32 ounces of milk each day. Expect the baby to take about 3-4 ounces per feeding, although this can vary. The most important number is how much your baby consumes over the course of a day.

You might be heading back to work during this first month, so now is a great time to discuss feeding responsibilities with your partner. A lot of bottle-feeding families like to have set feedings for dad to bond with the baby and give mom a break. If your partner plans to go back to work, this is especially important. For example, taking over a nighttime feed is a great way to not only bond with the baby but also help your partner during this recovery stage.

**Breastfeeding**: If your partner is exclusively breastfeeding, it can be hard to gauge how much milk the baby receives, but if your partner nurses every 2 to 3 hours, this should equate to 32 ounces. Just as with the first few days in the hospital, your baby's output is the best way to tell if the milk supply is adequate, so keep those diapers coming.

A month might seem like plenty of time for your partner to get the hang of breastfeeding, but it's very common for first-time moms to take several months to really feel comfortable with nursing. Not only that, but during this first month, your partner will also still be recovering from childbirth.

Depending on the length of maternity leave, your partner may start feeling anxious about breastfeeding and returning to work. If she is returning to work soon - or if she feels overwhelmed with on-demand breastfeeding - now is a good time to start pumping. Most hospitals will rent out breast pumps for new moms, so discuss this with your doctor.

Remind your partner that she doesn't need to worry too much about output at this point. Breastfeeding on its own is challenging enough, and it can also take a while to get the hang of pumping. She should start with one pumping session in the morning when milk supply is highest, then gradually add in sessions.

## SLEEPING

If there's one thing to be grateful for during your newborn's first month, it's that he will sleep a lot. Don't worry about sleep schedules at this point - just try to rest and sleep when your newborn sleeps.

This first month is also a great time to get a feel for your own parenting sleep style. Some parents struggle to sleep with the baby next to the bed, for example, while others can't sleep if they aren't within arm's reach of the baby.

One study suggests that mothers who breastfeed tend to sleep better with baby close by, so keep this in mind if your partner is nursing. The same study found that newborns slept an average of 14 hours per day, regardless of whether they were bottle-fed or breastfed. So take advantage of that time to get some shut-eye!

## BONDING WITH BABY

The word "bonding" might summon up saccharine images of dads and newborns gazing lovingly into each other's eyes - and this might not quite capture the entirety of your experience as a new dad. But bonding is so much more than a lovey-dovey activity that makes you and your baby feel good. Study after study has shown that bonding is *biologically necessary* for your baby's growth and well-being - and even for your own.

"When fathers are more engaged in caring for their babies, they experience stronger hormonal and neurobiological changes than when not engaged. These changes are, in turn, associated with short and longer-term benefits for the baby." (Fisher, 2018)

"Fathers have innate biologically-based abilities to bond with and care for babies; these are especially important for the health and safety of babies in situations of stress and risk." (Fisher, 2018)

These are direct quotes from a study published in the *Journal of Neonatal Nursing*. Researchers studied the effects of paternal care on high-risk infants in a neonatal unit. They found that the babies who interacted with dad regularly gained more weight and took to breastfeeding more easily than those who did not.

This is just one instance of evidence that bonding with your newborn helps your baby adjust to being outside the womb.

## LEARNING

Believe it or not, the first lesson your baby will learn - and perhaps his most challenging - happens this month. This is the fundamental lesson all human beings have to learn in order to survive: how to consume food.

It's easy to take this for granted but think about the life your baby has had up to this point. She's been floating around in mom's uterus without a care in the world, receiving everything she needs to grow without having to fight for it. What a life!

And then suddenly in that event we call "birth," everything changes. Now she has to work for everything. Her surroundings are completely changed. She feels the air on her skin and sees light for the first time. Her food is no longer magically transported into her body via the umbilical cord. Now she has to work for it.

Learning to eat is your baby's big task this month. It might sound crazy, but your most important task as dad is just to make sure she eats. Walking will come in time.

## KEEPING BABY SAFE

Newborns don't move very much, so take advantage of this month and do some childproofing around your house (if you haven't already!). These projects include:

- Checking all smoke and carbon monoxide detectors to make sure they work or installing new ones if necessary
- Reset the water heater to no more than 120 degrees Fahrenheit to avoid making baby bath water too hot
- Check bookshelves and other heavy furniture to make sure it's anchored to the wall (you'll be glad you did this when your baby is pulling up on things!)
- Put baby-proofing plugs in electrical outlets. Again, this won't be a concern for a while, but might as well get a head start!

The most important baby-proofing item on your checklist should be to make sure your newborn sleeps safely. Remove any excess pillows, blankets, or stuffed animals from your baby's crib, bassinet, or other sleeping space. Make sure there are no gaps between the mattress and the frame and that all screws are secured.

## HOW IS MOM?

Your partner might start to feel antsy around three weeks postpartum (if not sooner!). Reassure her that taking this time to relax, sleep as much as possible, and bond with your baby will help her bounce back faster in the long run. Study after study has shown this to be the case!

For example, a 2021 study on active-duty Army moms found that taking an extra six weeks (twelve weeks total) to recover from childbirth had the same level of physical fitness as Army moms who only took six weeks off.

You would think that at such an elite level of physical fitness, every week missed would count. But on the contrary, moms who allowed their bodies 12 weeks to recover matched the moms who took off six weeks and even *exceeded* their performance in several areas.

The takeaway? Women who took 12 weeks of maternity leave, as opposed to 6 weeks, did *not* demonstrate lower fitness scores one year postpartum when compared with those who took less time - and in some areas, their scores were better!

Rest is easier said than done, though, and it's easy to overdo it at this stage. Here are a few concerns your partner might have in this first month, and how to respond to them:

1. **Concerns about bleeding:** It's very normal for bleeding to last 4-6 weeks, or even longer. If your partner passes any large clots or feels like she is passing an abnormally high amount of blood, be sure to consult her physician.
2. **Concerns about low milk supply/baby's weight gain:** Again, new moms often fear they're not producing enough milk. Remind your partner of the baby's tiny tummy size (about the size of a large egg at this stage).
3. **Concerns about c-section incision:** Your partner might still be very sore if she had a c-section, and she might feel anxious about infection or other problems with her incision. It might also be hard for her to breastfeed comfortably. Encourage her to rest as much as possible and give it time. My partner loved using a breastfeeding pillow after her c-sections to help provide support while nursing.
4. **Concerns about pain:** If your partner is used to muscling through every illness or discomfort, she might feel annoyed about the need for pain relief. Most women use pain medication like ibuprofen or acetaminophen for the first few weeks postpartum or even longer if they had a complicated delivery. Your partner can also try other pain relief tricks, like a hot water bottle, heating pad, or - even better - a gentle massage from dad.
5. **Concerns about being "good enough":** A lot of first-time parents struggle with that nagging feeling that they just don't

know enough to be a good mom or dad. If your partner is having a challenging recovery, this is even more likely. Try to find opportunities to compliment her and give her positive feedback. The words "I'm proud of you" are music to a new mom's ears.

## HOW IS DAD?

In all the excitement of bringing your baby home, supporting your partner in her recovery, and possibly returning to work, it's normal for dads to feel a little neglected. A 2021 study published in the *Journal of Affective Disorders* found that one in ten dads of infants displays symptoms of mental health disorders. So if you find yourself feeling not quite yourself, you're not alone.

That same study also uncovered one big risk factor for mental health disorder symptoms: lack of sleep. The authors wanted to know whether dad's answer to one question - "How are you sleeping?" - could predict symptoms of depression, anxiety, and other conditions. The result? Dads who responded to this question negatively had a much higher chance of mental health disorder symptoms.

I'm not bringing this up to alarm you or make you feel like doomsday is near. Lack of sleep isn't inevitable, and for some dads, the first month of their newborn's life is relaxing and not stressful. But for many, it's a challenging time, and that's okay. The most important thing is to communicate with your partner and let her know how you're feeling. Or reach out to a family member, friend, or medical professional to help you get through this time.

If you're like most parents you'll spend a lot of time oohing and aahing over your newborn during this first month. Newborns are almost like totally different kinds of creatures. It's crazy to think we all started out this way!

# CHAPTER 5
# GETTING THE HANG OF IT

> "I cannot think of any need in childhood as strong as the need for a father's protection." – Sigmund Freud

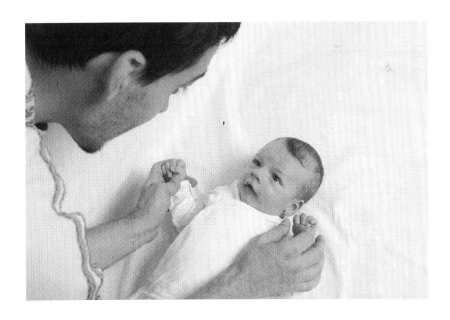

| Your Baby's Milestones: Months 2 and 3 | | | |
|---|---|---|---|
| Eating | Sleeping | Motor Skills | Language |
| Eats 4-6 ounces per feeding<br><br>Goes through a growth spurt<br><br>Might start cluster feeding | Sleeps an average of 14-17 hours per day<br><br>Sleeps on his or her back<br><br>Might go through a sleep regression | Still has newborn reflexes such as startle, rooting, stepping, and grasping reflex<br><br>Shows neck control, might start to roll from back to side<br><br>Tracks objects with eyes | Responds to facial expressions<br><br>Starts to smile<br><br>Coos and vocalizes |

# MONTH 2

THE FIRST MONTH has already passed, and you're starting to get the hang of things - and so is your baby. You'll probably notice your little one coming out of his shell a little this month. Here's what to expect during month two of your baby's life.

**Feeding**

I remember when our third baby was about six weeks old. My partner was at her limit with breastfeeding. "I just don't get it," she would say. "Just a few days ago, he was pretty much sleeping through the night, and now he wants to nurse every thirty minutes!"

At that moment, a light bulb went off. I remembered that our other two kids had done the *exact same thing*.

"Didn't this happen last time?" I asked.

After reviewing our mutual accounts of past history, we realized that yes, this had happened last time. And also the time before that. This caused us to do some additional research, and all sources ended up pointing to the same thing:

**Cluster feeding.** It might sound scary, but it's not. Or at least it's not *too* scary.

Cluster feeding happens when babies are going through a growth spurt. Basically, their little bodies say, "I want to eat ALL THE TIME." But fortunately, they can only keep that up for a few hours.

The solution for breastfeeding moms is to nurse on demand for a few hours while the baby is hungry so you all can get some well-earned sleep once the cluster-feeding session is done.

The good news is, if you can survive the nursing marathon, the baby will often get a deep snooze at the end. And that means you and mom can, too.

My number one recommendation? Find a Netflix show you both like and are willing to binge-watch while mom nurses the baby. I'm actually not joking. Passing the time in a fun way is key to success.

## Sleeping

Your baby might be sleeping longer stretches at night, especially if she is cluster feeding right before falling asleep at night. Then again, she might not - it really varies.

You'll probably have a lot of people asking if your baby is sleeping through the night. Don't get discouraged if she's only sleeping a 4 or 5 hour stretch. At this age, that is considered "sleeping through the night" by doctors and child development experts! Generally speaking, over a 24-hour period, you should expect your baby to sleep 14 to 17 hours.

If you're still on paternity leave, don't forget what I told you last month: sleep when the baby sleeps whenever possible!

**Bonding With Baby**

Bonding with your baby this month is all about eye contact and communication. Newborns are pretty easygoing during the first month - they kind of just eat, sleep, and poop. In the second month, they begin to look around, verbalize, and respond to their environment a lot more (as described in the next section).

This month, bond with your baby by talking to him and making faces at each other. It sounds ridiculous, but it's actually pretty addicting when you see your little guy responding!

Tummy time is also a great opportunity for bonding time, and the 2-month mark is a great time to start since your baby is probably showing a lot more neck control. Schedule a daily bonding session/tummy time - it will help your baby's development while also giving you guys time to get to know each other.

At this early age, tummy time is pretty simple:

1. Place the baby on his tummy on your chest, ideally skin-to-skin.
2. Talk to your baby and smile at him while he attempts to lift his head and look in your eyes. It takes a lot of effort!

Tummy time can be exhausting for your little guy, so start with a few minutes and work up from there. He'll build a bit more strength each month with your help!

**Learning**

You might have noticed your baby is a little more interactive this month. It's very normal for babies this age to begin vocalizing (i.e., cooing or making other cute baby noises aside from the initial crying and grunting sounds).

Your baby's senses have made leaps and bounds in the last month. This month, he will become much more responsive to noise, light, and motion. It's a pretty amazing process to watch!

Eye contact is also a huge factor in baby's brain development. Here's what researchers have to say about what babies can gain just by looking into their caregiver's eyes:

"Babies who gaze into their parents' eyes also receive key social cues that help to speed the next stage of language learning—the understanding of the meaning of actual words. Andrew Meltzoff of the University of Washington has shown that young children who follow the direction of an adult's gaze pick up more vocabulary in the first two years of life than children who do not track these eye movements." (Kuhl, 2015)

Here are a few other exciting learning moments to look out for this month:

1. **Recognizing facial expressions:** You might notice your baby responding to your facial expressions this month. For example, if you make a dramatic samurai face, your baby might raise his eyebrows or - if you're lucky - coo in delight. Pretty great!
2. **Tracking objects:** Newborns aren't very good at watching individual objects. This month, your baby will start to be able to follow slow-moving objects with his eyes.
3. **Sending clearer messages:** Your baby will start to communicate a little bit better this month, now that he's starting to use his hands more. For example, he might start bringing his hands to his mouth when he's hungry or wants a pacifier.

Reading your baby's signs is one of the most exciting things about being a dad. There's something really amazing about being able to tap into your child's needs and meet them faster and better. But of course, it takes some trial and error.

My advice is not to miss out on these very early moments of communication. You'll remember them forever. I still make fun of our oldest because the only way she would be calmed as a newborn was if I blared reggae music and walked around our house holding her in the football position. I'm still pretty proud of those dad skills.

**Keeping Baby Safe**

Not much new is happening in the way of childproofing this month. Two-month-old babies are still relatively immobile. However, your baby is probably moving around a lot more, so stay vigilant about creating a clear sleeping space. Remember, months 2-4 are the riskiest when it comes to SIDS, so safe sleep is crucial.

**How is Mom?**

Now that your partner may be feeling more mobile, you might be tempted to back off on offering to help. But this is one of the best times to offer some additional help so she can take an occasional break.

Ask if she wants you to hold the baby at a certain time each day while she goes for a walk. Or better yet, if your baby takes a bottle, volunteer to take over one feeding so mom can have a little alone time. Having a little alone time - even if it's just ten minutes - can give her the opportunity to relax, reflect, and recover from childbirth.

A quick note: If other people have offered help and your partner has turned them down, don't assume she would respond the same way if you made the offer. It's normal for new moms to be on the protective side, but you have already earned her trust by being with her through pregnancy, delivery, and the first month. So don't be afraid to offer help, even if she doesn't seem willing to take it from others!

**How is Dad?**

If you're like the average dad in America, you've probably been back at work for a while now. (The average paternity leave in the U.S. is only one week.) And if you're like me, you might be struggling with that.

After my first daughter was born, I was back at work after eight days. Since my partner had a c-section, her recovery took a bit longer. I tried to be supportive and positive, but honestly, I was pretty frustrated about returning to work so soon. All I really wanted to do was hang out with my partner and new baby daughter. At the same time, I was totally exhausted by the time I got home from work, so I felt a little worthless in terms of help with cleaning and helping my partner.

We got through it, but it was hard. But years later, I learned about something I wish I had known at the time: postpartum doulas.

A postpartum doula comes to your home to help with newborn care. Overnight postpartum doulas come at night to take care of the baby so you and your partner can sleep. She or he will also complete basic household tasks, like dishes, laundry, or organizing baby clothes...all while you sleep.

How had I never heard of this before?

If you're struggling with the postpartum period, I highly recommend looking into postpartum doula support. They can be a bit pricey, but it's totally worth it. Doulas in training will also often work at a lower hourly rate, so if you're on a budget, consider hiring a doula in training.

The second month definitely has its ups and downs. Everyone is adjusting rapidly and it might seem overwhelming at times. Lean on your partner for support - she understands better than anyone else what it's like!

## MONTH 3

Think about this: just 90 days ago, you hadn't met your baby. Now he's smiling, cooing, and starting to get mobile. Month three might be my favorite month of a baby's first year. Here are some things to look out for.

**Feeding**

Your baby's stomach has grown rapidly over the last three months. When your baby was three days old, her stomach's capacity was one ounce, max. At three months, her stomach can hold six ounces at a time. That's a pretty dramatic increase!

Three months is also typically a growth spurt period, which means your baby might need to eat more than usual. So if you notice she's taking more formula or breastfeeding a lot more than usual, you're not crazy!

Growth spurts are a regular occurrence in your baby's first year of life. Here are some signs that indicate your baby might be going through one:

- Increase in fussiness
- More frequent waking at night
- And of course, more eating!

It can be tough to get through growth spurts, and if your partner is exclusively breastfeeding, it can be especially challenging for her. Just remember - this too will pass! Thankfully, growth spurt periods usually only last a few days. And once this one is over, most babies don't have another one until the six-month mark.

## Sleeping

A lot of parents start thinking about sleep schedules for their babies around this time. There's definitely nothing wrong with starting to work towards a schedule, but just remember that there are still a lot of changes going on, so you'll want to be flexible.

In fact, you might want to hold off on sleep training altogether at this point, since three months is a classic time for babies to go through a sleep regression. What does that mean? Let's say your baby has been sleeping for five-hour stretches for the last month. All of a sudden, he's awake every two hours. Not only that, but he doesn't seem to nap as much during the day. This is a classic case of sleep regression, and it's very common for it to happen right around three months of age.

So why is this happening? For one thing, as noted above, your baby is probably going through a growth spurt. It's normal for sleep regressions to occur alongside growth spurts.

But there's another reason: your baby's sleep cycle is changing. Specifically, your baby is developing what we adults know as "circadian rhythm."

Circadian rhythm is basically a fancy way of describing the human body's 24-hour cycle. (Fun fact: the word "circadian" comes from the Latin "circa diem," which means "around a day.") When your circadian rhythm is thrown off, it can cause all kinds of problems, from digestive issues to depression.

It takes about two months for your baby's circadian rhythm to develop. When you hear people talk about newborns "having their days and nights mixed up," they're kind of correct - except that newborns don't really have a sense of day and night at all! Around the third month, your baby will transition to a more dependable sleep/wake cycle. Although baby sleep needs are different from adult sleep needs, you'll notice that he tends to be more awake during the day and sleeps more at night.

But before that magical moment, there is a transition period - and transitions can be challenging. The 3- or 4-month sleep regression so many parents know is a mark that this transition is happening. Your baby's chemistry is going through a huge change, and it can cause things to seem like they're getting worse.

But it's also the case that things will get better. Just when you've thought you can't take one more night of this, your baby will suddenly sleep a five-hour stretch. Hang in there! This too will pass.

**Bonding With Baby**

Who doesn't like a good massage? This month, take some time to learn basic baby massage techniques. Baby massage has been shown to reduce colic, improve sleep, and aid in growth and development. Here are a few simple baby massage tips to try this month:

- Gently massage baby's feet as she is falling asleep
- Place baby on her tummy and gently rub her lower back
- Wear baby in a newborn wrap and gently massage her back and feet while walking

Some experts recommend using a baby oil when you massage your baby, but it's not totally necessary. If your baby is extremely awake or active, wait a while before trying massage. You want to choose a time when baby is relaxed and ready to fall asleep!

Not only does infant massage help with common newborn challenges, but some studies also suggest it helps with father-baby bonding. It's a win-win!

**Learning**

We talked about the bonding benefits of tummy time last month, but I didn't really touch on some of the developmental advantages of regular tummy time. Science has studied this pretty thoroughly, so there's quite a bit of evidence out there!

Here are some of the ways tummy time has been proven to benefit your baby, as concluded by a 2020 study of over 4,200 participants:

- Prevents brachycephaly (a condition that results in a flattened head and requires treatment)
- Improves gross motor skill development
- Reduces body mass index/BMI
- Improves ease of crawling and rolling

So keep up your daily tummy time sessions - they're not only great for bonding but also for your baby's development!

**Keeping Baby Safe**

This month you might notice your baby starting to roll from his back to his side. This is the beginning of a new parenting stage: trying to keep up with your baby's ever-increasing mobility.

For now, the biggest childproofing item to keep in mind is preventing your baby from taking a fall. For example, up to this point, you may have occasionally set the baby down in the middle of your bed or on a sofa. Not anymore. All those signs on the diaper changing tables about not leaving the baby unattended are about to get real. You would be surprised how quickly a baby this small can move!

Always keep a hand on the baby on a high surface, and make sure the crib rails are correctly installed. The risk of SIDS and suffocation is still very real at this age, so even though it might be really tempting to put some of the baby's favorite toys and stuffed animals in the crib, hold off. It's not worth the risk!

Keep in mind that like any milestone, rolling doesn't *have* to happen this month. In fact, a lot of babies don't start rolling to their side for another month or two. But regardless, you'll be ready when it happens!

. . .

### How is Mom?

It's been three months since your partner gave birth, and you might assume things are totally back to normal "down there" for her. But if she's like 35 percent of new moms, she might be dealing with urinary incontinence. Or if she's like 20 percent of women who have given birth for the first time, she may have severe pelvic floor injury that would greatly benefit from treatment.

You would think new dads would hear more about this, but sadly, most dads I know are totally unfamiliar with these very common issues women face. Regardless of what type of delivery, birth is really hard on a woman's pelvic floor. It's important for your partner to know these issues are normal and that there are things she can do to recover and regain control.

Here are a few red flags to look out for. If you hear your partner mention any of these issues, encourage her to see her doctor. It's early enough that she can prevent a lot of problems down the road!

- Pain or a feeling of "bulging" in the pelvic area
- Loss of urinary control
- Loss of control of passing gas/feces
- Pain during and after intercourse

And speaking of intercourse, if she still isn't ready, be patient - especially if the birth was complicated or if she had stitches. Estrogen levels - which contribute to arousal - also drop significantly in the first months postpartum, even more so if your partner is exclusively breastfeeding. Encourage your partner to discuss any concerns with her physician to make sure there aren't any more serious and treatable problems.

### How is Dad?

Postpartum depression (PPD) happens to dads, too. A 2019 study found that fathers were most likely to experience PPD between three and six months after the baby's birth. The researchers analyzed over 20,000 subjects and concluded that postpartum depression in new dads is "relatively common." Keep in mind that although dads are more likely to experience PPD if their partner is going through the same thing, this isn't always the case.

Here are some of the most common manifestations of PPD in dads:

- Irritability
- Extreme mood swings
- Indecisiveness
- Depressed mood and a feeling of hopelessness
- Insomnia
- Weight loss/gain or changes in appetite
- Loss of focus
- Suicidal thoughts
- Social withdrawal

If you experience these symptoms, be sure to speak with your doctor and seek help. Although PPD can resolve on its own, it tends to be a sort of landslide condition - if you ignore it too long, it can get much worse very quickly. Keep in mind that you are more likely to experience PPD if you have had depression before, if the pregnancy was unintended, if mom is suffering from depression, or if there are relationship difficulties.

Between growth spurts, feeding challenges, and your partner's recovery, the third month is quite a hurdle. Congratulations on getting through! The next months will bring better sleep, more cute baby moments, and increased confidence in your role as dad and partner.

# CHAPTER 6
# NEWBORN TO INFANT

> "Son, brother, father, lover, friend. There is room in the heart for all the affections, as there is room in heaven for all the stars." —Victor Hugo

| Your Baby's Milestones: Months 4 and 5 ||||
| --- | --- | --- | --- |
| Eating | Sleeping | Motor Skills | Language |
| Might show signs of solid food readiness<br><br>Still needs around 24 ounces of milk per day | Sleeps about 15 hours per day<br><br>Might be ready to start sleep training<br><br>Discontinue use of inclined sleepers | Starts to put objects in mouth<br><br>Starts to hold head steady - might sit with support | Plays peekaboo!<br><br>Might start to laugh |

# MONTH 4

I HATE to break it to you, but your little baby is no longer a newborn. As of month four, he or she has been upgraded to the next level: infant.

The good news is, infancy is full of really great milestones. A few things to look forward to: solid food, non-gas-induced smiles, laughter, and more mobility. Here's what to expect in month four.

**Feeding Baby**

A quick Internet search reveals that there's a lot of debate out there as to when is the best time to introduce solid foods. My personal opinion (which has changed through the years as we've had more kids): Rule #1 is to *watch your baby*. If you see any of the following signs, it might indicate your baby is ready to start eating solid foods:

1. Your baby can hold his head up and sit with little or no support. (This one is a prerequisite, so don't move on if your baby doesn't have this down.)
2. Your baby doesn't have any feeding issues and can swallow easily.
3. Your baby gets frustrated and antsy when you and your partner eat. He might fuss or even grab at your food (be careful! He's more agile than he seems!). It's almost like he wants what you have. Chances are, he does, and it's time to show him the ropes.

Here are my top three starter foods to feed your baby if you decide to start solids this month:

**Oatmeal:** Oatmeal is my favorite first solid food. It's a great source of fiber, magnesium, and iron and is easy to prepare. Mix it with breast milk or formula. When the baby starts eating other fruit purees, I like to mix it in with oatmeal for the added fiber content.

**Rice cereal:** This is the classic first baby food for a reason. It's easy to feed your baby and is also relatively flavorless, so if you mix it with breastmilk or formula your baby is likely to enjoy it.

**Avocado:** Avocado is rich in healthy fats which have been shown to aid in your baby's brain development. Plus, it's just about the easiest first food out there. Simply slice a ripe avocado in half, scoop out a few tablespoons, and mash it up. Mix it with some breast milk or formula until it has a cereal-like consistency, then spoon-feed it to your baby.

Aside from breastmilk or formula, you don't need to add anything else to these foods, such as sugar or salt. Keep it simple!

Here are some instructions for successful baby feeding:

1. Prep your space. Have a damp washcloth or some paper towels on hand, as well as a baby bib.
2. Get baby ready. If it's warm enough, just take the baby's clothes off, down to the diaper. Easier cleanup that way!
3. Secure the bib around the baby's neck.
4. Get ready for his first bites! Make sure he opens his mouth to receive the food. You can lightly place the spoon on his bottom lip to encourage him to "Say ah!"
5. Feed the baby with a small baby spoon. It's totally normal for it to take a while for your baby to learn how to swallow food, so don't worry if he spits most of it up. At this point, there's no rush, and the amount of food your baby eats isn't important, since breastmilk or formula is the primary source of nutrition at this age.

It's also normal for feeding time to be messy, so be prepared to do some cleanup! I like to have a warm washcloth ready so I can give the baby and high chair a good wipe-down right away. No one likes cleaning up dried baby food!

**Sleeping**

You might have heard that your baby will sleep through the night once you start feeding solids. As much as I wish this were the case, research is still up in the air.

However, there was a promising study of over 1,303 babies in the U.K in 2018 that suggests early introduction of solids might actually help your baby (and you) sleep better. In the study, some of the babies were introduced to solid foods at four months, and others at six (the recommended age in the U.K.)

This is a summary of their findings:

"In a randomized clinical trial, the early introduction of solids into the infant's diet was associated with longer sleep duration, less frequent waking at night, and a reduction in reported very serious sleep problems."

Yes, you read that right - not only did introducing solids at four months help baby sleep longer and better, but it also correlated with fewer "very serious sleep problems" in caregivers. Sounds like a win-win!

However, keep in mind that if your baby isn't ready for solids, you probably won't see these benefits. In fact, it could backfire. So always go back to rule #1: watch your baby, and act accordingly.

**Bonding With Baby**

If you feel like you've got diapers, swaddling, and holding your baby mastered, it's time to consider another great dad bonding trick: baby wearing.

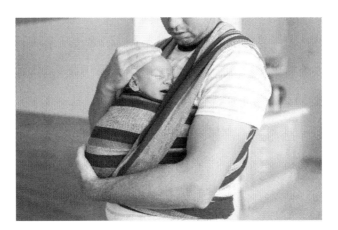

Baby wearing is exactly what it sounds like: attaching your baby to your body via a baby carrier and "wearing" him or her around the house, neighborhood, or wherever you happen to be.

When I first became a dad, baby wearing was just gaining popularity - with moms. Not dads. Now it's totally mainstream and normal to see dads toting their little tykes in a Baby Bjorn. I like to joke with my younger siblings and tell them I was the OG Baby wearing Dad.

In all seriousness, though, baby wearing is great for two primary reasons:

1. It encourages bonding
2. It can be really convenient

The second reason is only true if your baby likes being in a baby carrier. If your baby does not like being swaddled, he or she might not like being worn in a carrier. But it's still worth a shot!

Keep in mind that most standard baby carriers require a newborn insert for babies less than seven pounds. Wrap-style carriers are ideal at this stage, but personally, I found them challenging to use. Buckle-style carriers are much easier to take off and put on. They also offer great support for both the baby and the caregiver.

Here are some pro tips for successful baby wearing that won't be a pain in your neck (literally).

1. Make sure you keep your baby snug against your chest. I often see people wearing babies on the lower third of their torso - this is incorrect and could result in serious back pain. Also, it's less ideal for your baby since her head is less stable in this position. Don't let the baby hang off your torso. She should be snuggled in close and supported.
2. Keep the baby's legs in a frog or M-shape position, with the knees bent.
3. Don't wear your baby facing out just yet - her hips and legs are still developing, and this could put too much stress on her muscles.
4. Never wear your baby while you are cooking or doing other potentially hazardous activities.

It can be a bit tricky to get your baby comfy in the carrier the first few times, so make sure you have a helper nearby to assist if needed.

Not only is baby wearing great for a baby's feeling of security and comfort, but science suggests it's also beneficial for caregivers. For example, in a recent study, researchers investigated the effects of baby wearing on parents whose babies had a NICU stay. They found that baby wearing reduced parental feelings of stress and anxiety and increased feelings of parental empowerment. Pretty amazing!

## Learning

This month, it's time for your baby's four-month checkup! The pediatrician will be checking the following:

- Weight, height, head circumference measurements
- Physical exam - check for reflexes, color, muscle tone
- Updated vaccines - your baby will probably receive round 2 of the recommended vaccines for this age. These are typically DTap, polio, and Hib.

The doctor might also ask if your baby is sitting with support yet. Although this usually starts around four or five months, don't stress if your baby isn't quite there. Head control should be slowly stabilizing at this point, however.

Before your baby's checkup, take some time to sit down and write out any questions you might have for your pediatrician. I can't tell you how many times my partner and I have responded with a deer-in-the-headlights look when the doctor asks if we have any questions, only to remember a whole list a few hours later!

## Keeping Baby Safe

Now that your baby is able to put things in his or her mouth, it's time to do a quick check around the house for chokeable items.

Small objects under 1.5 inches in diameter are among the most common choking causes at this age. These might include buttons, bottle caps, coins, Legos, cough drops, peanuts and chewable vitamins. It might seem unlikely that your baby would encounter one of these items, but it's amazing how many small objects wind up on the floor or in baby's reach.

One team of researchers recommends the following test for whether or not an item is a choking hazard. Take a toilet paper roll and see if the object passes through it without any resistance. If so, the item is considered chokeable.

And of course, make sure to never give your baby any foods that could cause choking. Hot dogs, peanuts, popcorn, and grapes are some of the leading culprits.

**How is Mom?**

At this point, your partner may be feeling ready to get back to exercise - even if that just looks like a walk around the block. But there's something you both should be aware of before she resumes exercise: diastasis recti, or separation of the abdominal muscles.

Diastasis recti is a separation of the muscle called rectus abdominis - in laymen's terms, the six-pack muscles. This condition is extremely common after pregnancy and affects 60 percent of women who have had children. It usually resolves on its own after eight weeks, but 40 percent of women will still experience symptoms after that point.

Diastasis recti results from the high amount of pressure the growing uterus places on the abdominal muscles. During pregnancy, the layer of tissue between the six-pack muscles stretches and thins out. Sometimes, it becomes stretched a bit too much, resulting in diastasis recti. This usually happens in the third trimester.

If your partner experiences any of the following symptoms on a regular basis, she should be assessed for diastasis recti:

- A bulging in the abdomen, just above the bellybutton
- Difficulty lifting objects
- Pelvic pain
- Incontinence
- A feeling of weakness in the abdominal region
- Heartburn and indigestion
- Pain during intercourse

You might notice these symptoms are similar to the ones we discussed in chapter five. That's because the pelvic floor and core musculature work together. Core stability problems often go hand-in-hand with pelvic floor problems, and vice versa. And when you think about the changes your partner's body has gone through in the last year, it makes sense that childbirth often contributes to these issues.

Women with diastasis recti should avoid the following exercises:

- Crunches/sit-ups
- Plank
- Pilates core exercises
- Burpees
- Mountain climbers

Basically, she should avoid any exercises that put pressure on the abdominal region. Exercises like plank use gravity to strengthen the core - which is why they are great core exercises! But only if your abdominal muscles aren't separated.

The good news is, diastasis recti usually resolves without a lot of intervention. If your partner's abdominal separation is severe, she would probably benefit from physical therapy. My partner had diastasis recti after our second child was born. Although it was definitely not pleasant, with patience it resolved after about six months. This was eleven years ago, and it was difficult at that time to find someone to help her with it. Fortunately, awareness surrounding diastasis recti has greatly increased since then.

Encourage your partner to discuss diastasis recti with her healthcare provider and get an assessment, especially if she is planning to resume exercise soon. Although it's not an extremely dangerous condition, unresolved diastasis recti can lead to long-term problems like pelvic floor disorders and back pain.

**How is Dad?**

Most women return to work around this time, so you might be feeling a little added pressure if that's the case. Make sure to take time to do something you enjoy, be it a hobby, physical activity, or just watching your favorite sport and some friends.

If your baby care responsibilities have increased because your partner is back at work (or for any reason!), try to brainstorm ways to have fun while taking care of the baby. For example, I'm a pretty social person by nature and enjoy getting together with friends. After our babies were born and my partner started working again, I would have a few friends over on the weekend to watch soccer. This worked out well because I could easily supervise the baby while also hanging out with friends.

I always feel like the end of month four is kind of like coming out of a tunnel. Life is getting back to normal, and your baby is becoming less mysterious every day. It's amazing to see their little personalities slowly emerge!

## MONTH 5

By month five, your baby is feeling less like a fragile doll and more like a chunky little human. At this point, most babies have more than doubled their birth weight. Think about that for a minute: can you imagine doubling your body weight over the course of a five-month period? Probably not a very pretty mental picture!

This month your baby will continue to pack on the pounds, and will become a lot chattier. This is also a good time to start thinking about sleep training.

**Feeding**

You might notice your baby is feeding less frequently as you move into the fifth month. Your baby's stomach has grown a lot, so she's able to take in more milk at feedings. This also translates into fewer diaper changes!

Keep watching your baby for signs she is ready to start solids. If you've already gotten a start in month four, you can add on to your baby's food choices this month.

Here is a list of some great starter foods to feed your baby in month five, assuming she has already started eating solids. If not, go back to month four and start with those suggestions.

**My Top 3 Fruits for 5 Months:**

- Apples: Babies love applesauce. Apples are high in vitamin C which helps your baby's immune system.
- Bananas: Bananas are easy to prepare on your own, and also available as ready-made purees. Bananas can be constipating, so I like to pair them with oatmeal which provides fiber to help ease your baby's digestion.
- Pears: Pears have a slightly sweet flavor and are also high in fiber.

**My Top 3 Vegetables for 5 Months:**

- Sweet potatoes: Sweet potatoes are always our babies' favorites. They're also a great source of carbohydrates for healthy energy and easy to prepare at home.

- Green beans: I'm always surprised at how much our babies enjoy pureed green beans. This classic baby food is packed with vitamins A, B, and C.
- Carrots: Carrots are an excellent source of vitamin A, and their slight sweetness makes them a baby's delight.

As you can see, this month, we are adding some fruits and veggies into the mix. These are great sources of dietary fiber (which is important because it prevents constipation), as well as micronutrients like vitamin C, vitamin A, and the B vitamins. They're also easy to mix with foods your baby is already eating to make the adjustment easier.

Be sure to wait a few days after you give the baby new food. For example, if you introduce bananas on a Monday, wait until Wednesday to offer sweet potatoes. This gives the baby a chance to get used to the new foods and also allows you to observe whether or not the food settles well with her. Remember, breast milk or formula is still the only food your baby really needs at this point, so if she doesn't seem very excited about solid foods, don't fret.

If you observe any of the following signs after introducing a new food, discontinue feeding it until your baby is a bit older and consult with your doctor:

- Hives or rash
- Vomiting
- Swelling of the lips
- Wheezing or unusual sneezing

Seek medical help immediately if the baby has trouble breathing or swallowing.

## Sleeping

Now that your baby's sleep has become more regulated, it's time to start thinking about sleep training. There are so many sleep training methods out there, but in my experience, they really boil down to two big categories:

1. **Cry It Out:** For this method, you basically put your baby down at the desired bedtime and allow him to cry himself to sleep, or "cry it out." Proponents of this method note that while it can be hard the first few nights, eventually your baby will sleep through the night earlier and more successfully if you stick with it.
2. **Check and Console:** This method is similar, except instead of leaving the baby, you go in and make visits at regular intervals. Each night you gradually decrease the number of visits. My partner and I have used this method successfully with our children, and they are all great sleepers!

So what approach is best? It really depends. I would recommend researching different methods and choosing the one that clicks best with your personality and lifestyle. There are some great books in the References section that go in-depth on this topic.

Regardless of the method you choose, make sure it's right *for you*. You'll hear a lot of people throwing opinions around about sleep training, but ultimately the best approach is one that works best for you, your partner, and your baby.

## Bonding With Baby

Establishing rituals goes hand-in-hand with sleep training, but I've put this in the bonding section because I believe it's something parents might take for granted. This month is a great time to start to develop routines with your baby. Not only will routines make big life changes like sleep training and going back to work easier on the baby (and you and your partner!), but they also encourage better bonding for a simple reason: babies who have routines and rituals feel secure and develop trust for their caregivers.

Think about it for a minute. Let's imagine you have a caregiver who's very nice but who has no structure in their daily routine. Every day is a new adventure and you never know what to expect. This sounds exciting, but it's just overwhelming for a tiny human being trying to adjust to life in the world.

Now let's take the same nice caregiver and add in routine. Every day at a certain time, the baby is fed, bathed, or put down for a nap. The baby quickly learns not only what the routine is, but also *who* the person associated with the routine is. Therefore, the baby learns to trust not just the schedule but the people responsible for it - you and your partner.

This month, try adding one routine into your baby's - and your - day. It could be something as simple as going for a 10-minute walk at the same time every day, or giving baby a bath just before putting on his pajamas. Not only will this help your baby feel secure, but it will also create a great space for bonding and togetherness.

**Learning**

I remember when my first child was born, I was very disappointed at how long it took her to figure out peek-a-boo. If you're in the same boat, I have great news. Your baby's sense of object permanence is pretty much worked out at this point, so there's lots of peek-a-boo in store for you.

Around the age of five months, babies figure out that just because something disappears from view doesn't mean it's gone. It might seem like a small thing, but this is a huge jump in brain development. And since your baby is also starting to smile and laugh, month five has some pretty fun moments.

**Keeping Baby Safe**

Your baby can probably roll at this point, so it's important to stop using any incline sleepers. Incline sleepers became incredibly popular, and for good reason - they are amazing at helping babies sleep, since they situate the baby in an upright position. This helps especially with issues like GERD.

Unfortunately, incline sleepers have decreased in popularity just as fast. In 2019 Fisher Price recalled the Rock 'n' Play after over 30 infant deaths related to the product were reported, which shocked the parenting world. The Rock 'n' Play had been the gold standard of baby sleepers for about a decade, up until this point.

Incline sleepers are especially dangerous once the baby starts rolling. If you have one and have been using it up to this point, don't panic, but be aware that most pediatricians do not recommend using them for sleep. We have an old Rock 'n' Play that we received as a gift before the recall, and still use ours to put the baby in from time to time if we're nearby and the baby is in our sight. But the Rock 'n' Play or any incline sleeper should never be used as a sleeping space. The danger of entrapment has been shown to be high, especially for babies who are able to roll.

**How is Mom?**

If your partner is going back to work this month, she may be feeling overwhelmed, sad, or even guilty. Be sure to check in with her frequently and give her positive moral support. Reassure her that she's doing a great job.

Here are five simple things you can do to support your partner when she returns to work:

1. Take over dinner for a few nights of the week if you haven't already. That might mean cooking, or it might mean ordering takeout.

2. Arrange for a surprise date night. Ask a close friend or family member, or a babysitter you trust, to watch the baby for a few hours while you take your partner out for some R&R.
3. Take over some cleaning tasks, or hire someone temporarily to help out with cleaning the house. This way, your partner can come home and focus on spending time with you and the baby instead of cleaning.
4. Visit her at work on her lunch break with the baby, or any time it's possible. Or if that's not possible, send her photos if you're home with the baby.
5. Give her a lot of support if she is pumping. She might feel anxious about not providing enough milk or even struggle to pump at first. Ask how you can help her make the process as simple as possible.

Remember that the return to work is a big adjustment, and it might take a few weeks for everyone to get in the groove. Remind your partner often that you are there for her and the baby - just hearing this reassurance means a lot!

If you are planning to put your baby in daycare or hire a nanny, make sure you allow plenty of time to find a caregiver you really trust. I remember when my partner went back to work after our third child was born, and she wasn't totally happy with our childcare situation. After a few weeks, she seemed really down, so I asked a trusted family member who had offered help if she could take over just for a couple of days. It was amazing to see how much this relieved stress for my partner and made me realize how critical it is that you have the right care provider.

**How is Dad?**

Remember when we were talking about object permanence and how fun it is now that your baby can recognize objects aren't gone when they disappear from sight? Well, there's also a downside to your baby's newfound sense of permanence: she now knows when her parent leaves the room, and chances are she isn't very happy about it.

Gone are the days when you could simply hand your baby off to unfamiliar people at dinner parties and family get-togethers. Separation anxiety is very common at this age, and it can make life difficult.

Additionally, I remember being discouraged at this stage because our babies only wanted mom. Don't take it personally! Your baby is still attached to you, but it's common for babies to cling to mom at this age, especially if they are exclusively breastfed. Try not to get offended or interpret this as the baby not feeling secure with you.

Like all parenting challenges, separation anxiety fades away with time and it gets easier! For now, keep in mind that this is a normal stage and simply means your baby is growing up.

Between peek-a-boo, solid foods, and more consistent sleep, month five marks a huge jump in your baby's development. Before you know it, he'll be scooting around the house and getting in all kinds of trouble. Enjoy this stage while it lasts!

# CHAPTER 7
# HALF WAY THERE

 "In my career, there's many things I've won and many things I've achieved, but for me, my greatest achievement is my children and my family." —David Beckham

| Your Baby's Milestones: Months 6 and 7 | | | |
|---|---|---|---|
| Eating | Sleeping | Motor Skills | Language |
| Eats about 25 ounces per day<br><br>Takes 8 ounces per feeding<br><br>6-month growth spurt | Sleeps an average of 14-15 hours per day<br><br>Takes 3 naps per day | Starts to scoot/crawl<br><br>Enjoys board books | Responds to sounds/baby talk<br><br>Takes turns imitating sounds |

# MONTH 6

YOU'RE HALFWAY through your baby's first year! It might feel like your son or daughter has been around forever, or it might feel like only yesterday he or she was born. Chances are, it's a mix of both.

Your baby will go through a lot of big changes this month, and his or her personality will really blossom. Get ready for a fun month ahead!

**Feeding**

Typically a 6-month-old needs approximately six 6-8 oz formula feedings per day or about 25 ounces of breastmilk.

If your partner is breastfeeding, she might feel a little more at ease about nursing frequency for most of the month. But chances are, at some point, she will also feel like the baby is nursing more this month than last. That would make sense because most babies go through another big growth spurt right around the six-month mark!

If you forgot about growth spurts, go back to chapter five, where I discussed the common 3-month growth spurt most babies experience. The 6-month growth spurt will be more of the same!

If your baby is going through a growth spurt, he might go back to nursing every two or three hours. But once he's through the rapid growth period, things should calm down. Babies usually only need to nurse every three or four hours once they hit the six-month mark.

Your baby might seem extra fussy this month, and you might think it's food-related, but consider this: many babies start cutting teeth around the age of six months. If your baby seems frustrated and you know he has been eating and sleeping enough, you're probably dealing with incoming chompers.

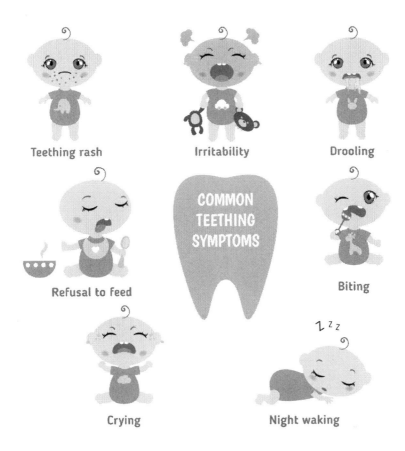

Here are a few common signs that your baby might be teething:

- Excessive drool
- Red gums
- Mild temperature (less than 100.4 degrees Fahrenheit)
- Pulling or rubbing ears
- Flushed cheeks
- Sleeplessness
- Fretfulness

Sounds like fun, right? Teething can be a challenging period for babies and parents, but there are a few things you can do to support your baby as he goes through this time. Try rubbing your baby's gums (with a clean finger, of course!) and letting him gnaw on your finger a bit. You can also purchase teething rings that you put in the fridge to cool. The cold offers babies a lot of relief from teething symptoms.

So what teeth emerge first? Watch the baby's bottom gums for the two middle teeth, which usually erupt around this time - or possibly later. The top two teeth will usually come in shortly after. However, each baby is different, so your little guy or gal might follow a different pattern. Likewise, it's hard to predict how babies will tolerate teething. Our third baby got all four of his first teeth in a week and barely even whimpered about it. Baby #5 took forever to cut her first tooth and was quite the drama queen. You never know!

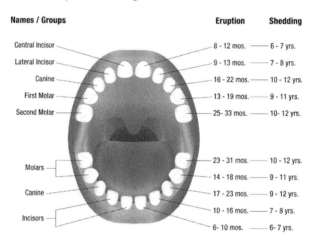

### Sleeping

Around six months, my partner and I always have a rude awakening. Just when we've gotten used to the baby napping at least three times a day, suddenly the third nap just disappears. Poof! Into thin air.

Here's another common scenario: you *thought* he was sleeping through the night, but now this month, the joke's on you. He's waking every two or three hours for the first time since his first week home. Between the lack of naps and the frequent waking, you might like your baby has once again decided to fool you.

If you find yourself in a similar situation this month, rest assured that it's totally normal. Your baby is going through a lot of changes in his sixth month, from growth spurts to teething, so it makes sense that sleep patterns would get a little wonky. Your baby is probably also a lot more mobile now, so he may just be rolling around and waking himself up! Try to hang in there and remember: this is just a phase. It will pass.

Speaking of being more mobile, you might find that even though you put your baby to sleep on his back, he ends up on his stomach. You don't need to disturb him and flip him back over - if he's strong enough to flip from his stomach to his back, it's okay for him to sleep on his back. But for the time being, keep putting him down on his tummy to start out.

A final note on sleep this month: expect your baby to sleep about 14-15 total hours per day. Usually, that's about two naps per day totaling 3 or 4 hours, and 10 or 11 hours at night.

**Bonding With Baby**

Bonding is all about communication, and your baby is probably becoming quite the chatterbox. Encourage his verbal skills while also strengthening your bond by talking back to him when he talks to you. At this age, babies love to hear themselves talk, but they love it even more when someone responds in baby talk.

Try this: the next time your baby starts babbling, try imitating it back to her. This might seem ridiculous, but studies have shown that speaking "baby talk" to your baby actually helps her learn the ins and outs of human language and develops her verbal skills. Plus, it teaches her to trust you. All that babbling going on in the high chair is, to her, a human dialogue when you join in.

So grab a cup of coffee, have a seat at the table, and take some time to chat. I can't think of a better bonding activity for this age!

**Learning**

This month your baby has his or her six-month checkup! In addition to all the usual items, your pediatrician will probably ask you about common milestones your baby has reached or will reach soon. These include responding to sounds, taking turns making sounds with you or another caregiver, reaching for objects, recognizing themselves in a mirror, or making basic consonant sounds.

If your baby hasn't met all these milestones yet, don't fret - but do be sure to mention it to your doctor at the appointment.

You might have noticed your baby has learned a major motor skill this month, if not earlier: pushing up with his arms. This might seem like a small thing, but it's actually a huge step toward crawling. Once babies can roll and push up with confidence, you can expect some variation of crawling to be right around the corner. Get ready!

**Keeping Baby Safe**

I know it's hard to believe, but your baby is probably on the verge of crawling. You might as well save the stress and childproof everything now, so you can enjoy watching her learn to crawl when it happens (it's pretty entertaining!).

You can continue to work on this as your baby gets older, but for now, there are a few simple things to accomplish:

- Make sure all electric cords are inaccessible or at least out of sight (for example, behind heavy furniture your baby cannot reach).

- Keep any space heaters, radiators, or other hot surfaces out of reach - you can block them off with baby gates if need be.
- Cover all electric outlets.
- Continue to keep items your baby could choke on off the floor or any other area your baby can reach.

First and foremost, keep the baby in your sight. It's fine for her to sleep in a different room, but when she's awake, she should be somewhere she can see you. Your dad intuition is better able to kick in when you have her in sight.

**How is Mom?**

If your partner is exclusively breastfeeding and your baby is going through a growth spurt, remember the tips I shared from month three. Encourage your partner to try pumping one bottle each day so you can help with a feeding or two - ideally at night or whenever your partner could most use the sleep. Growth spurts are hard on everyone, but when mom is the sole source of nourishment, they can be especially challenging for her!

Many women notice that their milk supply seems to drop around the 6-month mark. If your partner is concerned about this, she should consult with her doctor or a lactation consultant. There are a lot of things she can try if she wants to boost her milk supply, but make sure she has the essentials covered: a healthy diet, good hydration, and adequate sleep.

**How is Dad?**

I'll admit: I used to think the advice to enjoy the moment was pretty cliche and trite. But after years of doing this dad thing, I've softened my opinion. This first year with your son or daughter is going to fly by, and you can't get the time back.

Take some time this month to just be with your baby. Don't worry about hitting milestones, sleep schedules, or fine and gross motor skills - just enjoy his or her presence. That could mean taking a walk in nature, having some quality tummy time, or watching your favorite show together. You're halfway through the first year of life - soak it in.

The six-month mark isn't without its challenges (like all things parenting!), but just take it one day at a time. Oh, and if you remember - take lots of pictures. This stage has some pretty cute moments, from smiles to laughs, to really messy food moments.

## MONTH 7

Seven months in, you might be feeling a little anxious for your baby to be able to do more stuff. Rest assured, this month has a lot of fun in store. Before you know it, you'll be wishing your baby was a newborn again. I'm not going to lie: older babies can be a handful, but as I always say, it keeps you young.

**Feeding**

If your baby has been enjoying solid foods for the last few months, you can introduce a few new foods this month. Nutrient-packed vegetables like butternut squash, peas, and acorn squash are great options for purees, but you might also consider serving some of the baby's familiar foods as finger foods. For example, if your baby enjoyed avocados, you can serve them thinly sliced instead of mashed. Give it a shot and see how your baby responds!

Speaking of finger foods and baby feeding himself, you might have heard buzz about something called "baby-led weaning." This approach encourages parents to follow baby's lead when it comes to eating. At this age, that looks like putting a bunch of baby foods (prepared for safe eating, of course) on the highchair tray and letting baby go at it.

My partner learned about baby-led weaning when our first child was a baby, and we've been doing it ever since. Like any parenting philosophy, it has its pros and cons, but we've had an overwhelmingly positive experience. Here are just a few of the benefits we've seen firsthand in our own kids:

1. Leads to decreased pickiness. Our kids eat everything, and they've been that way since they started eating.
2. It's way more cost-effective. You don't have to worry about buying fancy baby food purees - just feed the baby simple foods you already eat.
3. Easier to control ingredients. I know exactly what my baby is eating. Given some of the questionable ingredients in commercially made baby food, that's really reassuring.
4. It's just easier. Personally, I find it much easier to dice up a banana in tiny pieces and put it on the baby's tray than it is to sit and spoon-feed.

The one big downside is that baby-led weaning is messy. Make sure you have a bib and some towels on hand for easy cleanup.

**Sleeping**

My partner was sick with mastitis (more on that below) around this time when our fourth child was a baby. She was so sick she couldn't keep up with the laundry, and I wasn't doing a great job supporting her in that regard, so at a certain point, she threw up her hands and told me to just buy the baby some new pajamas on the way home from work. That sounded like a good plan (less laundry is always good, right?), so I agreed it was the best idea.

But little did I know, the world of baby pajamas is more complicated than I realized! I had no idea there were so many options. As it turns out, finding the right pair of pajamas can be important if your little guy is picky about his pj's. Sadly, in my case, I brought home a 3-pack of footed pajamas, only to find out our son despises them and prefers a sleep sack. Lesson learned!

Here's a breakdown of three of the common types of baby pajamas:

**Footed pajamas**

These are the classic ones that have the feet attached. They are most commonly made with either zippers or snaps, although now there are even magnetic closure options!

Pros:

- These are convenient because you don't have to worry about your baby's feet getting cold.
- Footed pj's are also pretty simple when it comes to diaper changes.

Cons:

- Some babies don't like having their feet covered (case in point: my son).
- This sounds crazy, but there is a risk your baby could develop what's called a hair tourniquet, which is exactly what it sounds like: a piece of hair wrapped around your baby's toe that can cut off circulation. While footed pj's don't cause these, they can make it easier to miss them, so just be sure to check every so often!

**Sleep Sacks**

Sleep sacks are what they sound like: a big sack that your baby sleeps in. They usually close with a zipper. I like to use sleep sacks with a onesie underneath and a pair of baby socks (unless the baby doesn't like socks).

Pros:

- Sleep sacks give the baby a lot of room to move around, and allow you to decide whether or not to cover the baby's feet.
- The airflow helps the baby with temperature control at night.
- Some doctors recommend sleep sacks because parents are less likely to use blankets (which are still a safety hazard) when the baby is in a sleep sack.

Cons:

- Sleep sacks make diaper changes a little more complicated.
- Your baby might not like all the extra fabric.

**Sleep Gowns**

Sleep gowns are similar to sleep sacks, but instead of being closed in, the bottom is open and lined with elastic. They're super cute and usually long-sleeved, so you don't need any additional onesies, but a pair of socks might still be a good idea.

Pros:

- Sleep gowns make diaper changes very easy!
- Can be worn with or without socks.

Cons:

- Personally, I like sleep gowns for younger, less wiggly babies who aren't likely to move around and kick their legs out. This creates a lot of excess fabric at the top of the baby's torso, which isn't as safe (or comfortable!) as other options.

As with a lot of parenting topics, opinions abound as to what is the best type of pajama for babies. My opinion: the best option is the one your baby sleeps best in (provided that first and foremost, it's safe!). Understanding his or her sleep preferences will help everyone get more sleep - try to get to know them this month!

. . .

**Bonding With Baby**

It might sound crazy, but talking to your baby is one of the best ways to deepen your bond - and this month, he might even start to babble right back at you!

Multiple studies have found that babies whose parents speak to them from infancy go on to develop verbal skills more easily and may even have fewer academic difficulties later in life.

And while I'm on the topic, let's discuss "baby talk" - you know, that high-pitched way of talking adults always take on when they're speaking to infants or toddlers. I'll admit that before I became a dad, I couldn't stand baby talk, and I swore I would never talk to my child that way.

Like other ideas, this one also changed. Every time I talked to my daughter, I found myself speaking six octaves higher than normal. I don't recall ever making the choice to change my mind - it just happened. But one thing was clear: *she* liked baby talk. And once she hit six or seven months, she would even talk back, which was pretty awesome.

Believe it or not, there have actually been studies done on the benefits of baby talk - or "parentese" as it is sometimes called. Here's one amazing finding from some of her research:

"Parentese exaggerates differences between sounds—one phoneme can be easily discriminated from another. Our studies show that exaggerated speech most likely helps infants as they commit these sounds to memory. In a recent study by my group, Nairán Ramírez-Esparza, now at the University of Connecticut, had infants wear high-fidelity miniature tape recorders fitted into lightweight vests worn at home throughout the day. The recordings let us enter the children's auditory world and showed that if their parents spoke to them in parentese at that age, then one year later these infants had learned more than twice the number of words as those whose parents did not use the baby vernacular as frequently." (Boggs, 2017)

The shorter version: speaking to babies in their language helps them learn adult language faster. Pretty amazing! So keep up those lunchtime conversations - they're good for the baby's brain *and* for bonding!

**Learning**

When my oldest was about seven months old, I knew it was time. I ceremoniously sat her down on my lap, grabbed my delicate childhood copy of Maurice Sendak's *Where the Wild Things Are,* and began to read. I was so excited to finally share my favorite childhood story with her. After all, she was old enough to eat real food, so surely she could sit through a very short book.

By page three, I surrendered. She was trying to tear the pages and throwing a fit because I wouldn't let her.

Don't make the same mistake I did, but don't lose hope, either! While reading full-length children's books is a no-go at this age, board books are perfect for the six-month crowd. Select books that have high-quality, colorful images and not a lot of text. Remember: the goal is *not* to read your baby a story. The goal is to show her images of real-life objects she can learn to relate to. Now is not the time for Dr. Seuss, fairy tales, or, heaven forbid, Leo Tolstoy.

Here are some qualities to look for in board books at this stage:

- Simple, bright photos
- Good color contrast
- Not a lot of words

As you can see, it's best to keep it simple. And remember, your baby is not interested in a long-winded story. He'll be much more interested in grabbing, biting, and throwing the board books. That's why they're made of relatively indestructible cardboard, so it's best to just accept this reality and move on.

. . .

**Keeping Baby Safe**

My partner and I were getting a little frustrated. We were first-time parents living in a small apartment, and our daughter was into everything. She even started to throw massive fits when she couldn't open the drawers at her level. We couldn't even watch a 45-minute TV show or work on the computer in silence while she was awake. She was unstoppable and relentless.

In a stroke of genius, we figured out a new solution: instead of keeping our daughter out of all these spaces she wanted to explore, why not make them accessible and safe?

Your baby will be more and more mobile in the coming months - and her curiosity will also increase. Take a walk around the house and see if there are any spaces at her level that you could allow her to explore. For example, we moved all our lightweight, plastic dishes into a lower cabinet and put the kitchen appliances up high, then removed the child locks. Instead of having a screaming fit when she couldn't open the door, our daughter would entertain herself safely and learn all about Tupperware in the meantime. And my partner and I could eat dinner in peace. Win-win!

Of course, there are limits to this method, and it might result in more dishes, but if the baby's happy, everyone's happy!

**How is Mom?**

As your baby's feeding needs change and you introduce more solid foods, your partner might experience pain while breastfeeding. This might be alarming, especially if nursing has been smooth sailing up to this point.

There are a couple of common culprits when it comes to breastfeeding difficulties, but these are the big three:

- Clogged ducts
- Thrush

- Mastitis

Here's a bit of info about each of these problems, as well as some simple ways to alleviate the pain.

**Clogged Ducts:** This is basically a blockage that can occur when your partner stops nursing as frequently or is stressed or fatigued. It's common to get clogged ducts right around the return to the workplace, which may have happened recently for your partner. Clogged ducts are also common when the baby stops nursing as much as at night. Tight clothing and underwire bras can also contribute.

Clogged ducts are painful, but with sleep, hydration, and regular emptying of the breast, they usually resolve on their own. Encourage your partner to nurse as much as possible and take some time to rest. She can also massage her breast toward the nipple as she is nursing or pumping to encourage milk flow.

**Mastitis:** Mastitis is more commonly known as a breast infection. It's basically clogged ducts on steroids. In addition to the clogged duct symptoms, your partner will develop flu-like symptoms and generally feel horrible.

My partner has struggled with mastitis a lot in the past, so I feel like I have a good handle on it. Here are my top three tips for dealing with mastitis:

1. Don't Wait. If your partner has the symptoms of clogged ducts and also spikes a fever, she should go in right away so she can get on antibiotics promptly. If she waits too long, the infection could turn into an abscess.
2. Sleep and Hydrate. Encourage your partner to rest for a full day (at least!) and hydrate throughout the day.
3. Nurse as Much as Possible. The more she keeps the milk flowing, the less likely she is to develop a severe infection.

**Thrush:** Have you heard of yeast infections? The same fungus that is responsible for those nasty infections can cause another condition known as thrush. The name sounds scary, and I'll be frank: if you don't catch it early, it can be a little nightmarish.

The reason thrush is such a pain is that it often infects both the mom *and* the baby. It's also extremely contagious, so watch out for yourself.

The symptoms of thrush include nipple pain, red or peeling nipples, cracked or sore nipples, and a burning feeling while breastfeeding (or in general). Your baby might be unusually fussy, or he could have white patches in his mouth. Your partner might also have a vaginal yeast infection. As I said, it's not very pleasant!

If your partner or baby has recently been on antibiotics, thrush might be even more likely. You're also at higher risk if you have diabetes.

The good news is thrush can be treated with anti fungal medications. If your partner's symptoms last more than a week, she should consult with her physician.

One big tip for preventing all these conditions: practice self-care and try not to stress. More on that next.

**How is Dad?**

Just like your partner, stress relief is crucial for happy parenting. At this point, the science is undeniable: stress causes sickness, decreased performance at work, and increased rates of depression and anxiety.

Of course, it's impossible to eliminate all stressors from our lives. What you can control is how you respond to stress and how you take care of yourself. In the busyness of being a new dad, don't forget to manage your stress. How can you do that successfully? Here are a few ideas:

- Reach out to friends and family and get together. You don't have to stop socializing now that you're a dad - in fact, now it's more important than ever.
- Get out of the house. Go for a walk in nature, to a sports game, or just sit outside. Studies show that sunlight and a change in scenery go a long way in preventing depression and coping with stress.
- Seek counseling or professional help if you can't shake the stressed feeling. There's a fine line between stress and depression, and if you're experiencing the latter, it's important to get help.
- Be active. Physical activity is another great way to channel stress. If there was a type of exercise or sport you enjoyed before your baby was born and things got hectic, get back into it!

Most importantly, communicate with your partner. If you feel overwhelmed by stress, don't keep it to yourself. Not only is it bad for you, but your partner will probably notice you're not being open - with causes even more stress!

Despite the fun moments and baby laughs, months 6 and 7 can be a little challenging when you throw teething and growth spurts in the mix. Congratulations on making it through!

# CHAPTER 8
# READY, SET, GO!

 "Having kids is like living in a frat house -- nobody sleeps, everything's broken, and there's a lot of throwing up." -- Ray Romano

| Your Baby's Milestones: Months 8 and 9 | | | |
|---|---|---|---|
| Eating | Sleeping | Motor Skills | Language |
| Good time to introduce sippy cup<br><br>Drink about 24 ounces per day | Sleeps an average of 12-15 hours per day<br><br>Decreases to 2 naps per day instead of 3 | Throws things for fun<br><br>Might start to pull up on furniture | Babbles<br><br>Points to objects<br><br>Might be able to learn basic baby sign |

## MONTH 8

YOU'VE LEARNED a lot about your baby over the last two months, and you've probably also persevered through some challenging moments. Now it's time to get ready for crawling, pulling up on furniture, and playtime.

**Feeding**

Your baby will become increasingly independent at mealtime over the next few months, but make sure you're still there to supervise. In addition to the foods I've already discussed, here are a few items to add to the baby's menu this month:

- Yogurt (plain, made with whole milk)
- Dry cereal designed for babies
- Small pieces of tofu

This is also a great month to introduce the sippy cup. If your baby is already taking a bottle regularly, this should be a pretty smooth transition. If your partner is exclusively breastfeeding and the baby hasn't taken a bottle, it might require a bit of practice.

Here are some qualities to look for in a starter sippy cup:

- Easy for baby to hold
- Soft mouthpiece
- Spout that resembles a nipple for exclusively breastfeeding babies
- Spill-proof!

Breastmilk and formula should still make up the majority of your baby's calories at this age, but feel free to let your baby have water in the sippy cup. Hold off on cow's milk and juice for now. (If you're wondering, babies this age can have yogurt even though it is made from cow's milk because it is cultured, making it easier to digest.)

Finally, remember that if your baby doesn't take to the sippy cup right away, it's not a big deal. Most doctors don't recommend phasing out bottles completely until babies are twelve months old, so you still have time!

**Sleeping**

Once again, your baby might go through a sleep regression this month or next. As her body adjusts to eating solids, cutting teeth, and being more active - not to mention all the huge mental jumps her brain is going through - it's understandable that sleep patterns might become unpredictable.

For example, if your baby has been taking three naps up to this point, expect that to decrease to two at some point soon. As far as nighttime is concerned, don't be alarmed if your baby wakes much more frequently this month. In fact, it might be best to just get a head start and plan a night-time feeding/comforting strategy with your partner before the sleeping difficulties hit.

And of course, keep in mind it's okay for the baby to cry at night. But if you feel inclined to comfort him, that's okay, too. Giving the baby a sippy cup with some water to keep in the crib might help him self-soothe. Just avoid giving him juice or breastmilk, which can cause tooth decay.

**Bonding With Baby**

As I've mentioned before, communicating with your baby is one of the best bonding activities you can do at this stage of development - and for your child's whole life. Open communication builds trust between kids and parents, and it really does start from the beginning.

One way to communicate more easily with your baby is to learn some simple baby signs. Baby sign language certainly isn't necessary for your baby to learn, but in my experience, it can make things much simpler, especially at feeding time. My partner and I haven't used baby sign language extensively, but we do teach our babies the following five signs around this age:

1. "Drink": Make a cup with your hand and pretend to be drinking it
2. "Water": Tuck your thumb and pinkie in like you're making the number "3," then tap your chin with your index finger
3. "More": Babies are always quick to pick up on this one! Pinch your fingers against your thumb on both hands. With the fingers facing each other, tap both hands together repeatedly.
4. "Milk": Pump both hands like you're milking a cow. Yep, it's that simple.
5. "All done": Put your hands in front of you with the palms forward, the switch to palms facing you, and repeat.

And of course, this is a great age to start with the classic signs we all know, like "bye-bye" and "blow a kiss"!

**Learning**

There's a special moment that happens at this age, and it is really remarkable. Picture this: you're holding your baby, and she drops her toy on the ground. Not too exciting up to this point, right? You just pick it up and give it back to her and move on.

Not anymore. Now, if you pick it up and give it back to her, she'll probably throw it right back on the floor and squeal with delight. Your little girl has learned an entertaining activity: dropping things!

Once the charm has worn off, you might think your little one is dropping things just to drive you insane, but her motives aren't that sinister. She's really just honing a new skill, the same way she has been practicing pinching objects, picking things up, rolling, and babbling. Humans learn through repetition, and this month she's getting a great lesson in object permanence.

**Keeping Baby Safe**

If you've kept up with the childproofing tips so far, you should be pretty set this month. But if your baby is slithering, crawling, or doing whatever variation he likes best, you've probably noticed he's a lot dirtier than he was in his squeaky-clean newborn days! That's because he's spending a lot more time on the floor.

Here are some tips for keeping the floor safe and clean now that your baby is exploring every nook and cranny:

- Buy a robot vacuum - or put it on your wish list if you have family members who want to buy you a great, practical Christmas present.
- Lie a clean sheet down on the floor in the room where your baby is crawling or scooting around. Put the corners of the sheet under coffee tables or other heavy furniture to secure them in place.

- Dress your baby in pants or leg warmers to protect his knees and keep him cleaner.

You might worry that the floor is unsafe or too dirty for your baby. Rest assured, some research shows these initial floor-dwelling months are good for your baby's immune system and could even prevent asthma later in life.

**How is Mom?**

There's a lot of talk out there about babies who have separation anxiety, but not as many people realize that it can also happen to moms. One study by the Society for Research in Child Development found that maternal separation often peaks when babies are around this age.

Maternal separation anxiety is exactly what it sounds like: an intense feeling of worry, fear, or guilt when mom is separated from the baby. Your partner might also experience irritability, fatigue, and even physical symptoms like nausea, headaches, and panic attacks. It can be debilitating in severe cases, so it's important that your partner gets help if she has symptoms.

If your partner shows symptoms of maternal separation anxiety, communicate with her openly and non-judgmentally. Reassure her that it's normal to feel stressed and worried about the baby, but also suggest that she discuss her symptoms with her care provider. Counseling and medical interventions can make an amazing difference.

**How is Dad?**

If you haven't gone out on a date since your baby was born, now is the time. Your baby can probably take a bottle at this point, and might even be eating solid food. But even if that's not the case, breastfeeding frequency should have spaced out enough to go out for dinner with your partner.

That's all well and good, but there's probably a big question on your mind: who's going to watch the baby? If you don't have family or friends who could do it, ask around about trusted babysitters. Make sure you get a chance to meet the sitter beforehand since this will allow you and your partner to be more at ease.

When date night comes around, have the sitter come about 15 minutes before you want to leave so you can show her around the house, explain any feeding needs, and show her exactly how you put the baby down. The trick with babysitters is to keep things as normal as possible, so give the sitter a full debrief of all your routines.

That's a wrap on month eight. Hopefully, you've enjoyed a date night with your partner and maybe even learned some baby sign language with your little one. On to the last three months of year one!

## MONTH 9

Your baby has officially been outside the womb as long as he or she was inside it. A lot can happen in just nine months! Nine months might actually be my favorite baby stage - and not just because nine is my favorite number. Your baby is really blossoming, and now that you've gotten through some of the growth spurts, teething struggles, and general insecurity of new parenthood, you'll love watching the changes take place.

**Feeding**

This month is a great time to start putting utensils on the baby's tray. Your baby is probably already showing interest in using the same dishes, spoons, and forks as mom and dad, anyway. I remember our fourth child refused to eat unless his highchair tray was set in the exact same configuration as mine and his mom's!

Before I go on, here is a disclaimer: just because you give your baby a spoon and fork does not mean he or she will be able to use them. In fact, it will probably be quite some time before the baby is eating with utensils in a civilized way. So don't put away the bibs and spill mats just yet!

That said, allowing the baby to practice - or really, play - with utensils during meal times is a great way to encourage fine motor skill development. Here are some tips for getting started:

- Buy utensils that are designed for young babies. The best materials are silicone or BPA-free plastic (metal is a bit heavier and best for when the baby is older). The utensils should be light enough for the baby to easily hold, and they should be much smaller than normal utensils.
- Serve foods that won't be too frustrating for the baby. The best foods are ones with a thicker texture that doesn't slide off the spoon, like mashed chickpeas or mashed sweet potatoes.
- Prepare for messiness. Lots of messiness. Once your baby figures out how to get the food on the spoon or fork, don't be surprised if he would rather draw on his tray than actually eat. Expect most of the food *not* to make it into his mouth.
- Keep the servings small. (See previous note - the less food you serve, the less mess!)

As for plates, personally, I prefer to skip them. There's a much higher chance the baby will actually throw the food *out* of the highchair zone if you serve it on a plate. Just put a tablespoon or two directly on the highchair tray, hand the baby his utensils, and let him have some fun.

Looking for new foods to add to your baby's repertoire? We usually introduce meat around the nine-month mark, and it always goes over well. Shredded chicken and ground beef are some great options. Just make sure the meat is well-cooked and then allowed to cool enough for your baby to handle.

## Sleeping

My one important note this month: check in with your baby's crib mattress. If your baby is starting to pull up on furniture (more on that below), it's probably time to lower your baby's mattress. Once your baby can pull up on furniture that is about eye level, it makes sense that the guardrail should be higher than that.

Another note: if you've been co-sleeping with your baby until this point, this is a good time to introduce a separate sleeping space. Try a co-sleeper that fits up next to your bed, or put a crib next to you.

Finally, my last word of advice is to trust your parental instincts. Different parents feel different ways about sleeping arrangements at this point, and for good reason: we all have different situations regarding work, sleep, and emotional status. Take all these factors into account as you choose the best solution for your family.

## Bonding With Baby

To this day, one of my favorite ways to bond with my oldest child - now age fourteen - is by playing games. We love to go to a nearby board game cafe and check out a few board games to play. There's something about games that provides the perfect bonding opportunity: problem-solving, laughter, and friendly competition.

Of course, at this age, competition isn't really a factor, but playing games with your baby is one of the best ways to bond. It's surprising how much a nine-month-old baby can actually participate in play. Here are some fun games to try with your little guy or gal:

- **Peek-a-boo:** The classic, and for good reason - babies love it!
- **How big is baby:** Say, "How big is [insert name here]?" And then reply, "Soooo big!" while waving your hands in the air.
- **Chase the baby:** Pretend to be a bear and chase your baby around the room while pretending to eat her toes.

- **Hide the toy:** Same object permanence concept as peek-a-boo, but with a toy.
- **Dance party:** Turn on music and dance around the room.

The interactive aspect of play makes it a great bonding activity, but as a bonus, it's also amazing for your baby's brain development. As usual, the things that help your baby bond with you also help with physical and neurological development. It's a win-win for both of you!

### Learning

This month, it's time for your baby's 9-month checkup. In addition to measurements (no vaccines at this appointment if you've kept up so far), your pediatrician might ask about the following developmental milestones:

- Can your baby sit without support?
- Does your baby grasp objects and get mad if an object is taken away?
- Does your baby crawl or stand while holding onto a stable object/person?
- Does your baby mimic you?
- Does your baby point to indicate what she wants?
- Does your baby babble? (Make consonant sounds like "mama," "baba," and "dada"?)

### Keeping Baby Safe

In addition to all the physical and neurological changes your baby is going through this month, you might also notice a big step: cruising. This basically means your baby will start pulling up on furniture (she may be doing this already), then walking from side to side, using the furniture as support.

This might seem like a small thing, but it's a huge step! Walking could be just around the corner, or it could still be quite a way off. Either way, it's important to encourage this important stage of development and also keep your baby safe. Here are some tips:

- Get ready for some spills. Now that baby is upright, it's inevitable that he or she will have some falls. Don't beat yourself up if and when it happens!
- Make sure all your furniture is secured to the wall. Babies will pull up on anything within reach, and it's easier than you might think for furniture to tip!
- Get on baby's level - literally. The best way to find safety hazards is to crawl around the house and inspect everything at the baby's eye level. Remove any dangerous objects as you come across them, and secure any furniture that might be hazardous.
- Follow your baby. When in doubt, just put your baby down on the ground and observe what she does for about thirty minutes. This will give you a good idea of what you might need to babyproof.

Your baby's increased mobility is exciting, but it can also be a little nerve-wracking. Remember, when your baby is in sight, you're doing all right. But for the moments you or your partner can't be present, it's reassuring to know your home is safe for exploration.

A final note: if your baby isn't cruising yet, don't worry. As I've said before - every baby is different! In the meantime, it doesn't hurt to get a head start on babyproofing since it could happen at any time.

**How is Mom?**

The 9-month mark seems like it would bring freedom from the effects of pregnancy and childbirth, but that's not always the case. If your partner feels discouraged that she isn't "back to normal" at this point, you can both rest assured that this is totally normal.

Whatever you do, don't trust the Internet, which will tell your partner she should "bounce back" between 6 and 12 weeks (that was like, 6 months ago, right?) While she's probably not dealing with any of the more acute postpartum symptoms - the ones everyone talks about, like bleeding, engorgement, pelvic floor soreness, or post-cesarean abdominal scar healing - there are likely to be other lingering effects of what her body has gone through over the last eighteen months. Some of these include:

- Difficulty losing weight
- Fatigue
- Stretch marks
- Saggy skin on her belly
- Leaking urine during high-impact activity
- Discomfort during intercourse

While these symptoms are normal, they can still be disheartening. Encourage your partner to discuss any concerns with her care provider, and give her lots of affirmation if she is struggling. Nine months might seem like a long time, but childbirth is a demanding process that requires more healing time than what the common opinion dictates.

**How is Dad?**

Around this month, I start establishing a routine with my kids. If there are periods of time when I'm the sole source of entertainment (and, of course, food), I try to get the baby excited to spend time with me. I know that sounds kind of sad, but if Mom needs to leave the house, it can be hard to convince the baby to be happy!

Now that your baby is more interactive, I have a word of advice: start to build your "dad bag." This is a bag (or actually, I use a plastic bin) of toys, random objects, and snacks that only come out when it's my turn to babysit. When your partner has to work on weekends, and you're home with the baby, you can bring out the dad bag, and rest assured your baby will be quickly distracted from mom's absence.

Some ideas for things to put in the dad bag at this age:

- Finger foods the baby doesn't usually get (for example, I have a few containers of puffed cereal and some applesauce pouches)
- Electronic toys that the baby doesn't play with often (my partner can't stand electronic toys - her loss!)
- Sensory blocks
- Some dad-time board books that we always read together

This is a trick that will work throughout most of your baby's early childhood. Our "baby" is now 18 months old, and I still have a dad bag for days when my partner has to work, and we don't have childcare. Give it a try!

Nine months postpartum is hopefully less difficult than nine months pregnant - but no matter what, you're making it through this first year and getting to know your baby (and your partner) as you go. Not to mention, you've probably learned a few new things about yourself.

# CHAPTER 9
# BYE BYE BABY

 "Until you have a son of your own, you will never know the joy, the love beyond feeling that resonates in the heart of a father as he looks upon his son." – Kent Nerburn

| Your Baby's Milestones: Months 10 and 11 | | | |
|---|---|---|---|
| Eating | Sleeping | Motor Skills | Language |
| Eats about 16-24 ounces per day<br><br>Eats most simple baby foods<br><br>Might start to wean off bottle | Might cut back to one long nap per day<br><br>Sleeps about 14 hours per day | Starts to cruise<br><br>Sees an object across the room and goes to it | Can say "mama" or "dada"<br><br>Points to objects when you name them |

## MONTH 10

ONCE OUR KIDS have hit the ten-month mark, I feel like they have a very limited amount of time left as a baby. Toddlerhood is just around the corner, and the last three months of the first year are a time of remarkable changes. Here's what to expect from your little one this month.

**Feeding**

At this point, your baby can eat pretty much anything, but you should still hold off on the following foods:

- Cow's milk
- Honey
- Dried fruit and nuts
- Raw vegetables and fruits that pose a choking hazard
- Highly processed foods that are high in sodium and sugar

Just like most things in your baby's life, creating a meal schedule for your baby will help establish consistent, healthy habits. It also makes it easier for you if you need to leave your baby with a caregiver. Here's a sample menu for a 10-month-old, along with some health benefits for each food.

**Breakfast:**

- Scrambled egg: An amazing source of protein, healthy fats, and nutrients
- Banana: Great source of potassium and healthy carbohydrates

**Lunch:**

- Cubed, cooked sweet potato: Lots of fiber and vitamins
- Soft cheese: Cottage cheese is a healthy option that is rich in calcium

**Snack:**

- Yogurt (plain, made with whole milk): Full of probiotics for gut health

**Dinner:**

- Diced chicken: Good protein source
- White rice: Simple carbs that are easy to digest
- Applesauce: A healthy dessert!

As you can see, your baby eats most of the same foods you do at this point. You can keep things really simple by just feeding your baby the same meals you and your partner eat, if possible. Just make sure to dice any foods that might be a choking hazard and allow hot foods to cool completely before serving them to your baby.

**Sleeping**

Sleep habits tend to become a little more reliable from here on out - which is great news! Your baby might cut back from two naps to one long nap this month. Generally speaking, if your baby still naps two times per day, you can expect him to take the first nap after about four hours of being awake, then the second nap about three hours after the first. Bedtime should be about four or five hours after the baby wakes up from a second nap.

Your baby will probably nap for about two or three hours per day, with eleven or twelve hours of sleep at night.

Here's an example of what your baby's sleep might look like this month:

- 7:00: Wake
- 10:30 - 12:00: First nap
- 2:30 - 3:30: Second nap

- 6:30: Start bedtime routine (bath, read a book, change diaper, pajamas)
- 7:00: Bedtime

But remember, nothing is set in stone at this age and sleep patterns are variable, so try to be flexible and expect the unexpected!

**Bonding With Baby**

Now that your baby is becoming more and more independent, you might think you don't need to hold her as much. But physical contact and affection remain important ways to strengthen your bond. If your baby seems fussy, restless, or just plain grouchy, and you've tried food, sleep, diaper changes, and teething remedies, it might be that she simply wants to cuddle. Don't underestimate the power of snuggling!

Baby wearing can also come in handy here. My babies really enjoyed it when I wore them on my back at this age. This allows the baby to look out and see the world while he's awake and energetic and then rest his head on your back when he gets worn out.

**Learning**

Ten-month-old babies are extremely curious and usually pretty fearless too, which can keep mom and dad on their toes! Learning at this age happens primarily by engagement with all five senses, whether that be through play, eating, or just exploring. Here are some ways to engage each of your baby's five senses this month and help with his or her cognitive development:

**Sight:** It's hard to believe that just ten months ago, your baby could only see a few feet in front of her and was unable to track movement. Her vision has improved drastically since then, and now she can spot her favorite sippy cup from across the room and rapidly move to go grab it.

Engage baby's sense of sight by continuing to read board books with clear pictures (photographs are great at this age) and lots of color contrast.

**Sound:** You might have noticed your baby responding to the sound of music, or swaying to a good beat. Babies love music, and it's amazing for their brain development. A 2016 study showed that listening to music helps the baby's speech development. Pretty amazing!

You don't have to subject yourself to Baby Mozart, either. Our children have loved a variety of music at this age, from classical, to bluegrass, to reggae. Anything with a strong beat is sure to get baby dancing!

**Smell/Taste:** It's easy to take the sense of smell for granted, but it might be our strongest sense at birth. Newborn babies are able to recognize their caregiver's scent and recognize them, which compensates for the lack of vision in those early days.

The best way to develop a baby's sense of smell and taste is to expose him to a wide variety of healthy foods. Encourage him to smell his food before he tastes it. I've done this with all our kids, and it's amazing to see how much it helps them be comfortable trying new foods. When you're cooking, keep baby close by and give her different ingredients to smell, like garlic, onions, and herbs. You'll probably get some funny reactions!

**Touch:** The sense of touch is the very first sense to develop in the womb. At age ten months, your baby's sense of touch helps her learn about dimension and space. You might notice your baby touches your face if you sit face-to-face with her at a close distance. This is her way of getting to know you better, and it applies to the whole world (hence the need to babyproof everything!).

This month, encourage your baby to learn through her sense of touch by providing objects with different textures. Babies also love putting things in containers at this age and stacking blocks. It doesn't have to be fancy to be developmentally beneficial!

**Keeping Baby Safe**

Childproofing is important and good, but the best way to keep your child safe in the world is to teach them how not to get hurt. Up to this point, that's been pretty hard to do, but with your baby's new speech development, you can begin to teach him how to stay safe.

Babies of this age form strong associations between sounds and situations. Use this to your advantage when teaching your baby about safety. For example, when you're in the kitchen, point to the stove and say "Ouch" or "Hot" while making a serious (not mad or angry!) face. Or if your baby starts to crawl close to the stairs, don't just run over and pick him up. Instead, calmly pick him up and say "Ouch" in a stern voice, then explain why he shouldn't play by the stairs. These simple communications will instruct your baby about what is and isn't safe.

But of course, he is still a baby - so don't stop with the babyproofing just yet!

**How is Mom?**

I'll never forget something that happened after our first baby was born. She was around this age, and my partner was just recovering from a horrible bout of mastitis. She had been nursing literally around the clock and was totally exhausted. At one point, she seemed really down, so I asked if there was anything I could do for her. She thought about it for a minute and then said, "I think I just need to go on a walk outside for like, five minutes..by myself."

I thought she was joking at first, but then I realized that between taking care of the baby, resting, and working, she hadn't really had any time to just *be*. She was so caught up in all the items on the to-do list that she had literally forgotten about herself. I realized I needed to give her more space to do things she enjoyed, like being outdoors, reading, running, and gardening. I needed to make sure she prioritized her own needs.

Now that your baby is more independent encourage your partner to take some time for herself once a week. This could be going out with a friend, doing a hobby she enjoys, playing a sport, or any other enjoyable activity. The first year of motherhood can be hard for some women, as their sense of identity becomes more and more bound up with the baby. Taking time for herself will help her recharge and regain her sense of self.

**How is Dad?**

There's a lot of talk about when moms should start exercising after childbirth, but what about the dads? Like so many dads out there, you might have been so caught up in your new baby, work, and your relationship with your partner that you've let yourself go a little bit. Ever heard of "dad bod"? Yeah, it happens. But that's okay. It's never too late to get back to it!

If you're like me, you might find yourself interested in exercise for the first time in your life now that your baby is here. I wasn't into sports growing up, but after my daughter was born, something clicked. Suddenly I got into soccer, running, and weightlifting. This had a huge effect not only on my relationship with my baby and my partner but on my life. I was more confident and energetic and felt more in control of my health and well-being.

This month, why not try out a gym membership? Most gyms offer a free trial period that allows you to scope out the place and try any classes you might be interested in. Just like your partner, you have to make sure to carve out time for yourself, and a trip to the gym might be just the ticket.

Parenthood isn't just about the baby: it's about you, your partner, the baby, and your relationship. This month, try to slow down and enjoy these people you call family. Cancel some plans you've been dreading anyways, and stay home for a movie night with your people. No one's going to complain about that!

## MONTH 11

Next month, your baby turns one! If you're planning a birthday party, this is the month to get a head start on preparations. Take some time to sit down with your partner early in the month and nail down the following details:

1. Party date, time, and location
2. Guest list
3. Food or drink you will serve
4. Presents!
5. Invitations

It's best to send out invitations about two weeks in advance to give people plenty of time to plan, or three weeks if you are sending physical invitations. Even though the party isn't until next month, the more work you do this month, the more you'll be able to sit back and enjoy the day.

**Feeding**

It might seem like your independent guy or gal doesn't need breastmilk or formula anymore, but you should still be feeding 16 to 24 ounces per day. Aside from that, real food is increasingly the name of the game. However, some pediatricians do recommend parents start weaning the baby off the bottle at this age. That might seem like an impossible task, but with planning and consistency, you can do it.

Here are a few steps to weaning your baby from the bottle this month:

1. Offer the sippy cup for the baby's first feeding. If you catch him when he's hungry, he's more likely to take to the sippy cup.
2. Once you've successfully replaced the bottle for the first feeding, add in one sippy cup feeding per day. I like to switch off and on - so first feeding with the sippy, second feeding with the bottle, third sippy, etc.
3. Continue this pattern until your baby is completely weaned from the bottle.

Consistency is the key here. Your baby might not like it for a few days, but just like with sleep training, a consistent routine will produce good results. Make sure that you offer the sippy cup at the same time every day. And remember, this does not apply to nursing from the breast, which should continue for at least one year. We'll discuss this more below!

**Sleeping**

There's so much pressure in the parenting world for your baby to sleep all night, which can make parents feel like they're doing something wrong if their baby still wakes at night. Instead of obsessing over that long night-time stretch of sleep (as nice as it is when it happens!), try to get in touch with your baby's sleep habits. One of the best ways to do this is by keeping a baby sleep journal.

A baby sleep journal is exactly what it sounds like: a written record of when your baby sleeps and wakes. My partner and I have kept sleep journals at various points in our kids' lives - usually when we're having struggles. But even at non-challenging times, it's a great way to get a better sense of your baby's habits.

Keeping a sleep journal allows you to pay close attention to when your baby's waking hours are, and how long the stretches usually last. This can be a game-changer when it comes to baby sleep. For example, if your baby is fighting nap time (as babies often do at this age), try taking notes every day for a week about how long your baby tends to stay awake between sleep times. This will allow you to see if you might need to extend the waking window or not. If you discover you have been trying to put your baby down for a nap after a two-hour waking window, try waiting 2.5 or 3 hours and see if that makes it more peaceful. Sometimes, making these minor adjustments can make sleep much less of a struggle.

By age 11 months, your baby might not be sleeping through the night, but hopefully, you have at least gotten a better sense of a sleep pattern. If you still feel completely frustrated and confused by your baby's sleep habits, a sleep journal should get you on the track to feeling more in control.

**Bonding With Baby**

Continuing the trend from previous months, this month offers a lot of opportunities for the #1 bonding activity: communication. You'll notice your baby is gesturing a lot more to communicate his needs. For example, he might point and grunt at his bottle from across the room or toddle over to you and stretch out his arms to ask to be picked up. Whether you can fulfill his request or not, make sure you give him a response. This will teach him that he can trust you to listen to him and respond to his needs. It will also teach him *to* communicate in the first place!

Here are some other communication skills your baby might develop (with your help!) this month:

- Babbling in "conversation"
- Grunting in response to a question or to indicate a desire
- Pointing at objects
- Following simple directions
- Saying "mama," "dada," "baba" and other simple words

And there's another means of communication your baby might develop this month: the art of the temper tantrum. Don't be alarmed! I find the best way to calm a tantrum at this age is just to hold the baby and provide comfort while the baby calms down. It can be difficult to figure out the causes of tantrums at this age, so usually, removing the baby from the environment and providing some TLC will de-escalate the situation.

**Learning**

Develop your baby's language skills this month by naming objects and describing processes. She might not be able to say many words, but you've probably noticed that she understands a lot!

One of my favorite learning activities to do with my kids at this age was to take them on walks. Leave your phone at home and step outside for some fresh air and a little language exercise. Some of the simplest words to teach your baby - "sky," "tree," "bird," "airplane," "car" - are right outside your door. And of course, your baby will love the walking practice! If you can't get outside, you can also do this activity at the window. If your window faces a street, your baby will love watching the cars go by.

And of course, keep up the reading! At this age, your baby might even start to pick board books up and "read" them by herself. Again, even though she can't vocalize the words yet, her brain is absorbing so much, just with the visual stimulation.

Finally, encourage learning by posing a lot of questions. At mealtime, ask your baby if she would like one food or another. For example, "Do you want yogurt or cereal?" She might not be able to provide an answer yet, but she's on the way! This month she might even nod "yes" or shake her head "no" in response to questions. This is an exciting parenting moment - you can finally communicate a little bit more!

. . .

**Keeping Baby Safe**

Now that the baby is probably on his feet a lot more, make sure you always check the surfaces he is walking on. I remember one time I took my daughter to the playground and wondered why she wouldn't walk on the pavement. Then I realized it was super hot, and she was only wearing socks!

You might also consider getting some lightweight shoes for your baby to wear to protect his feet. Baby moccasins are a great choice because they stay on better than a lot of other options. At this age, your baby doesn't need tennis shoes with thick soles - in fact, the more flexible the sole, the better.

**How is Mom?**

If most of your partner's friends don't have kids yet, this can be a lonely time - especially if she is staying home with the baby full-time. Encourage her to look for local groups of parents that she can connect with. Not only will this provide your baby with a great opportunity for play dates, but perhaps more importantly, it will allow your partner to get some much-needed social time with other moms who understand the challenges and joys of raising babies.

If your partner has struggled with postpartum depression, this is all the more important. Research has shown that women are much more likely to experience postpartum depression when they don't have social support. There are many support groups that are designed specifically for moms who are working through postpartum depression, so encourage your partner to ask your local hospital or medical health professional for resources to get the support she needs.

**How is Dad?**

Low social support is also a risk factor for paternal postpartum depression, so my advice this month for you is the same as it was for your partner - find your people! Get together with a dad friend, or look for social support groups in your area if you feel the need to socialize. There are also many couple support groups that offer opportunities for friendship and support as you adjust to your life as new parents.

Even if you're not struggling with depression or other mental health symptoms, getting together with a friend can be a real fresh of breath air when you've been talking baby talk all day. So set aside some time this month for socialization!

Now that your baby is entering the early stages of toddlerhood, parenting becomes both easier and more difficult. On the one hand, your baby is more independent and not as reliant on you and your partner. On the other hand, there are a lot more decisions to be made! What parenting style is the best fit for you? What do you envision for your baby's education or activities in the future?

Of course, you have plenty of time to think about all this, but it's pretty exciting to see your little one's increasing personality and to imagine what he or she will be like at this time next year - not to mention five years from now.

## CHAPTER 10
# FIRST BIRTHDAY

 "Nothing ever fits the palm so perfectly, or feels so right, or inspires so much protective instinct as the hand of a child." – Gregory David Roberts

| Your Baby's Milestones: Month 12 | | | |
|---|---|---|---|
| Eating | Sleeping | Motor Skills | Language |
| Eats about 16-24 ounces per day<br><br>Can start to drink cow's milk | Sleeps an average of 13-14 hours per day<br><br>Takes at least one nap per day | Might start walking independently | Says "no"<br><br>Says at least one word that designates a specific object |

## FEEDING

At this age, one of the best ways to calm a restless baby is to put him in his high chair with his favorite finger foods. Then again, your baby might also start to show some signs of pickiness at this age. Just when you thought you had the least picky baby on the block, he'll start throwing what you thought was his favorite food yesterday on the floor today. Don't fret - it's classic! Just continue to offer a variety of nutritious, healthy foods about 3-5 times per day.

This month, your baby can finally try out cow's milk. Don't get too excited, though - a lot of babies can't stand it at first. Start with a very small amount - a tablespoon added to formula or breastmilk or formula is fine at first. Make sure your baby tolerates the milk well before you increase the amount. Here are some signs that he's not quite ready for cow's milk:

- Swollen lips, face, or eyes
- Itchy rash
- Digestive issues like vomiting, diarrhea, or cramping
- Runny nose
- Eczema
- Diaper rash

If your baby starts displaying these symptoms shortly after cow's milk is introduced, that might be a clue that it is related to the milk. Talk to your pediatrician about these symptoms before you continue to give your baby cow's milk.

**Sleeping**

Your baby seems like she's all grown up these days, but she still needs 13-14 hours of sleep every day. That usually looks like 2-3 hours of napping during the day and 10-11 hours of nighttime sleep.

Make sure you don't skip the bedtime routine at this age. Your little one has gotten used to the rhythm of each day, and even though she might fight bedtime more than she did last month, she really needs the ritual of a bedtime routine.

If you haven't sleep-trained your baby yet, you might wonder if it's too late. The answer is, of course not! Just keep in mind that many babies go through a growth spurt around this age, so it's normal for sleep patterns to be a bit off. This also might make it more difficult to sleep-train your baby, but with consistency, you will see results.

**Bonding With Baby**

Your baby might have learned a very important and fun word by now: "no." You might wonder how you're going to deal when she's saying no on a regular basis! A lot of parents start wondering about discipline at this age, and it's no wonder! Toddlers can be pretty stubborn and headstrong.

So why am I discussing discipline in the bonding section? Because discipline without bonding is a dead end. Forming a strong bond of trust with your baby is the first step in establishing effective discipline. This foundation of trust continues to be important through toddlerhood, elementary school, and even in the teenage years. It all starts now!

Here are some tips for successful discipline and trust establishment at this age:

1. Breathe before you react. Stop and take three deep breaths before you take action. This gives you some time to clear your head and respond in a gentle, loving way.
2. Establish boundaries. All that babyproofing you've done plays an important part in discipline from a young age since it establishes areas that are off-limits.
3. Be consistent. This is the hardest and most critical step, but experts agree consistency is key to discipline at any age.

Keep in mind that disciplining your child is an act of love. For me, it helps to think of discipline as instruction and teaching instead of simply bossing your child around.

**Learning**

Your baby will have her one-year checkup this month. In addition to the usual physical checkup items like vaccinations, height and weight check, and head measurements, your doctor will also ask you about the following learning milestones:

- Is your child saying any words?
- Does your child respond to simple instructions and the word "No"?
- Is your child pulling up on furniture and cruising?
- Has your child started walking yet?
- Does your child play simple games like peek-a-boo?

Generally at this age, your answer to most of these questions will probably be yes. Talk to your pediatrician at the appointment if you have any concerns about learning milestones or language development. Early intervention is key, so an open discussion will allow your care provider to address any problems early on.

**Keeping Baby Safe**

Now that your baby is bigger and more mobile, you might wonder if it's safe to move his car seat to a forward-facing position. Although the recommendation used to be one year, the American Academy of Pediatrics now recommends that toddlers stay rear-facing until they are at least two years of age.

To make your baby more comfortable, consider switching to a convertible car seat if you haven't already. Convertible car seats have a bit more space, making them more comfortable - especially for long car rides. Generally, it is recommended to switch to a convertible car seat when the top of your child's head is less than an inch from the top of his infant car seat or when she is 30 inches tall or 30 pounds. For most toddlers, this is usually between ages 1 and 1 ½.

Unlike infant car seats, convertible car seats do not have a base, so they're a bit more cumbersome. If you have a small vehicle, look for a compact seat to save space but also give your little one some more room to stretch out.

**How is Mom?**

Most women find that they are finally feeling more like themselves by the one-year mark, but this isn't always the case. If your partner has lingering problems due to pregnancy and childbirth, encourage her to take time to see her care provider this month. Specifically, if she has incontinence or other pelvic floor issues, discomfort at her c-section incision site, pain during intercourse, or if she is struggling to get back to a healthy weight, she should seek assistance.

**How is Dad?**

You've made it through your first year as a new dad - you deserve to celebrate! Schedule a time this month to have a one-year birthday date with your partner and toast all the ups and downs this year has brought.

### Tips for a Successful First Birthday Party

Last-Minute Preparations

You've probably already sent invitations and gotten started your birthday party preparations, but if not, here are some last-minute items to get ready for the big day:

- **Review the Guest List:** You've already sent the invitations, so make sure to sit down and review the guest list to make sure you've included everyone you want to invite. Reach out to

anyone who hasn't RSVP'd yet to see if they will be there for the big day.
- **Plan the Menu:** If you're serving food at the birthday party, you'll need to decide whether you will make the food yourself or outsource. Personally, unless you *love* cooking, I recommend outsourcing. Stores like Sam's or Costco have affordable party trays that will feed a crowd on a reasonable budget - and their items are pretty tasty, too! And don't forget beverages. Plan to get plenty of bottled water, and make a list of other beverages you want to serve.
- **Choose a Theme:** Choosing a theme for a party isn't just fun - it's also a great way to simplify things. Common first birthday party themes could be something related to baby's favorite toy or character (for example, a Winnie the Pooh party or a woodland animal party are popular options). Or it could be more abstract, like a color/pattern theme or food item (for example, pink polka dots or a fruit theme). Or you could choose something seasonal, like autumn leaves or a summer beach theme.
- **Select the Cake:** Once you have the guest list, menu, and theme selected, it's time to figure out the main event: cake! If you plan to host a large party, a sheet cake or two is ideal. For smaller events, you could serve cupcakes or even cake pops. If a lot of your guests have food allergies, plan to have a second cake available that is safe for them to eat.

### Tips for the Day of the Party

The big day has finally arrived! It's easy to get so wrapped up in the excitement - and yes, the stress - of your baby's party that you don't have the chance to enjoy yourself. Here are my top 3 tips for keeping party day fun for everyone:

1. **Be Strategic With Timing:** I always reassure new parents that they don't have to plan their life around the baby's sleep

schedule, but this day is an exception. Plan the party for the time of day when your baby is awake, happy, and hungry.

2. Get Help With Cleanup: Ask a few close family members or friends to pitch in with cleanup. Or if you have any responsible teenage nieces or nephews, offer them a small stipend in return for cleanup help. Not having to worry about cleanup will minimize stress and allow you to enjoy the party (and maybe even take a nap when it's over!).
3. Keep it Short and Simple: Of course you want to celebrate this event, but when it comes to birthday parties for kids this age, simplicity and brevity are key. Schedule the party for no more than a few hours, and keep the decorations simple and easy. You'll have plenty of time for more complicated party schemes when your little one is older and more able to appreciate the details!

Of course, you and your partner will want to celebrate as well. One of my favorite birthday parties we hosted was my son's second birthday party. We had a late afternoon party with four of our close friends who also had children of similar ages. After the party was over and the kids were tired out, we had a few trusted babysitters come to our house to take care of the kids for a few hours while the parents went to a baseball game, sans kiddos. The kids had a great time with each other, and it was pretty fun to celebrate the first year of parenting with our friends, too.

One other tip - if you expect a lot of your baby's similarly-aged friends to be at the party with their parents, be sure to have a changing station set up, as well as a quiet area where parents can take their little ones if they get overwhelmed. Not all babies are social butterflies, and they might need a break from the excitement.

Between checkups, birthday parties, and all the everyday busyness this age brings, the twelve-month mark is an exciting time. Congratulations on your baby's first year - it's a big parenting milestone for you and your partner, too.

# CHAPTER 11
# PARENTING STYLES 101

### WHAT'S *YOUR* PARENTING STYLE?

IN RECENT YEARS, there's been a lot of talk about different parenting styles or philosophies. With the rise of social media, it's easier and easier for people to share their opinions on the "best" way to raise your kids (for better or worse).

I like to tell a story about one guy knew who was totally stressed about being a new dad. As he and I were talking about it one day, he mentioned something about EC. I asked him what that was and he told me it stood for "elimination communication," which is basically a way of potty training your newborn right from the get-go.

Yes, you heard me right - he was trying to potty-train his newborn. No wonder he was stressed out!

As we kept talking, it became clear that he and his partner had been duped. They truly believed that by not following this ideology and practicing EC, they were dooming their child to a life of depression, health problems, relationship issues, and all kinds of other problems.

But the question they weren't asking was: how is this affecting my relationship with my child and my partner *now*? Is it more important that my 2-week-old baby poops in the toilet or that we're all getting enough sleep? Is following this parenting style and sticking with EC interfering with my mental health and that of my partner?

Don't get me wrong - I have nothing against anyone who practices EC. If it works for you, that's awesome! But clearly, it wasn't working for my friend.

This is just an example of the danger of clinging to a parenting style and its tenets without asking what is best for you, your partner, and your baby. Don't fall into this trap!

Instead, think of the first year of your baby's life as a time of discovery. Rather than adopting one parenting style dogmatically, remember that your ideas will grow and develop over time - and there's nothing wrong with that!

With all that said, let's take a look at some of the popular parenting styles out there.

## ATTACHMENT PARENTING

What It Is

Attachment parenting became widely popularized by pediatrician Dr. William Sears, whose book *The Baby Book* took the parenting world by storm. Attachment parenting is based on the idea that children need to connect with their parents early on in order to form a relationship of trust. This parenting style features the 5 B's:

1. Birth bonding
2. Breastfeeding
3. Baby wearing
4. Bed sharing
5. Being responsive

Today, attachment parenting is one of the most popular parenting styles, especially with new parents. I think a lot of this has to do with the wide body of literature Dr. Sears and other AP proponents have written about the first year of life. Whereas some parenting books are more appropriate for parenting older kids and teens, attachment parenting begins before the baby is even born.

Pros and Cons

**Pros:**

- Attachment parenting has been shown in studies to reduce stress in children and also help them regulate their emotions.
- There's lots of literature out there about attachment parenting, making it accessible and easy to learn about.
- Since attachment parenting focuses on following the baby's cues, it can result in less frustration - babies are fickle!
- Some parents find it less stressful to have the baby hang out with them all the time.

**Cons:**

- Following attachment parenting principles to a T is hard! Some parents may find baby wearing, bed sharing, and breastfeeding on demand to be impractical for their life situations.
- Attachment parenting doesn't give some parents enough space. You might feel overwhelmed if your baby is constantly with you.

## AUTHORITATIVE/PARENT-LED PARENTING

What It Is

Authoritative parenting (not to be confused with "authoritarian parenting," which is very different) was first developed as a concept by clinical psychologist Diane Baumrind in the 1960s. Authoritative parenting was the style she favored and put forth as the best. This parenting style combines setting firm limits through positivity. Unlike authoritarian parenting, which is often called "drill sergeant" style parenting, authoritative parenting supports the idea that while children need to observe boundaries, they shouldn't be coerced into following rules.

It can be hard to see how to apply these ideas during infancy. After all, authoritative parenting is all about communication - and your baby can't talk! However, as I've noted in previous chapters, getting to know your baby starts now. If you are attracted to the basic idea behind authoritative (also known as parent-led) parenting, you can see these first few years as a good practice run in patient communication and trying to meet your baby's needs.

Pros and Cons

**Pros:**

- Some children who are raised in a parent-led environment tend to be less likely to rebel and make harmful choices later in life
- Other studies show that parent-led approaches result in greater empathy and conscientiousness later in life

**Cons:**

- Hard to apply these principles during infancy
- This parenting style requires that parents take time to have an open dialogue with their kids - and as wonderful as that sounds, it can be challenging!

## FREE-RANGE PARENTING

What It Is

Free-range parenting became all the rage in many parenting circles after the release of Lenore Skenazy's book *Free Range Kids* in 2009. This excerpt from the book's introduction provides some insight as to the basic gist of what this parenting style is all about (it's actually a hilarious book - I recommend reading it!):

"Somehow, even those of us who looked forward to parenting without too much paranoia have become anxious about every possible weird, scary, awful thing that could ever, just maybe, God forbid!, happen to our kids - from death by toilet drowning to stranger abduction to electrical outlet cover ingestion. Yes, I just read that those little plastic things you stick in the outlets to prevent baby electrocution turn out to be potential choking hazards. Just *try* not to worry."

As the name of the book suggests, this style of parenting encourages parents to allow their children to be free from excessive amounts of scheduling, rules, and safety measures. It's a controversial style of parenting because sometimes it's hard to gauge how much independence is too much, and vice versa, but the overall emphasis on helping kids discover freedom and "just let kids be kids" is definitely popular. Not to mention, it's a bit refreshing to be able to take a step back as a parent and enjoy the simple act of watching your baby develop without worrying about whether he's on track or following all the rules.

It might seem like this parenting style is a better fit for parents of older children, but I find a lot of free-range parenting concepts to be helpful during infancy. For example, I remember when our oldest was a baby, I was hyper-vigilant about knowing when she was going to eat, sleep, meet new milestones, and everything else babies do. I would get frustrated when sleeping schedules that had been working for weeks would suddenly fall apart or when a routine we had been keeping up with suddenly became unsustainable.

I quickly realized so much of my baby's life is out of my control and difficult - if not impossible! - to plan in advance.

Free-range parenting wasn't a thing back then, but if it had been, maybe I would have been able to chill out a little bit more! The general impulse to allow children to grow and develop in the way that is best for them is my key takeaway from free-range parenting styles.

Pros and Cons

**Pros:**

- Encourages flexibility in parents as the baby goes through changes that are often unpredictable
- May reduce parental anxiety because it prepares you for the unpredictability of parenting

**Cons:**

- Some parents may need more structure than this parenting style advocates
- It's easy for free-range parenting to be misunderstood as permissive parenting, a.k.a., letting your child do whatever he or she wants, which can be neglectful on the parent's part.

## GREEN OR ECO-FRIENDLY PARENTING

What It Is

Green parenting, also known as eco-friendly or earth-friendly parenting, is a relatively new parenting style that has really only been developed in the last few years. As climate change has become more of a hot-button issue, parents have taken note and sought out ways to make child-rearing as environmentally responsible as possible.

This might sound like overkill, but the reality is clear: a lot of single-use products that have been proven to contribute to environmental decline are related to parenting. Case in point: disposable diapers.

Green parenting advocates a decreased reliance on single-use products and emphasizes a DIY approach to child-rearing. Here are a few common green parenting practices:

- Cloth diapering
- Making baby food at home

- Exclusive breastfeeding for at least 6 months
- Extended breastfeeding (breastfeeding beyond 2 years)

There really isn't a founder of green parenting - instead, it has emerged as a bit of a grassroots effort. Green parenting groups (also called natural parenting or ecological parenting) are very common on social media channels.

Pros and Cons

**Pros:**

- Environmentally sustainable
- Some practices - such as making baby food at home - could minimize your baby's exposure to harmful ingredients

**Cons:**

- Many environmentally-friendly practices (such as cloth diapering or making homemade food) are much more difficult and time-consuming

These are only a few of the many parenting styles out there. It can be a little overwhelming to try to keep up with all these ideas and approaches, but the one thing you *can* work on now that never goes away is consistency. Study after study shows that parents who are consistent in their approach are successful in the long run. Just like a dependable routine helps your baby feel secure and loved, consistency in your approach to parenting will provide a nurturing space for your child to grow and thrive.

But at the same time, keep in mind that your baby is still very young! It's not the case that you have to choose one of these parenting styles and stick to it for the rest of your life. I like to think of them as springboards. All these styles offer some good ideas (and maybe some not-so-good ideas) for you and your partner to ponder together. Your style ten years from now may be very different from the way it looks now. The most important factor is that you remain in open communication and work together to develop your parenting style.

# CHAPTER 12
# TAKING CARE OF YOUR RELATIONSHIPS

YOU'VE HEARD THIS BEFORE, but that's because it's true: the first step to solving any problem is admitting it exists. If you and your partner have taken that step, you are already on the way to improving your relationship.

If you haven't experienced relationship issues since your baby's birth, you're fortunate. Relationship issues are incredibly common in the first year postpartum. Couples who went through a traumatic birth experience are even more prone to difficulties, according to recent research in *Frontiers in Psychology Journal*. And if you or your partner suffers from postpartum depression, you are also at a higher risk of relationship problems.

Once you and your partner have agreed you want to work on your relationship, it can be difficult to know where to begin. I highly recommend couples therapy as a starting point. A counselor can evaluate you and your partner for signs of postpartum depression and provide treatment options, including talk therapy or medication. Even if you or your partner aren't diagnosed with postpartum depression, couples therapy is a great way to connect on a regular basis with an unbiased therapist who can help you sort through the challenges of new parenthood.

Aside from couples therapy, it's important to prioritize regular time together. Set aside time at least once a week to just be together or do something you enjoy as a couple.

## SELF-CARE AND WHERE TO FIND SUPPORT

In addition to spending quality time with your partner, there are two other aspects of nurturing your relationship that many people overlook. First is the need for **self-care**. That's exactly what it sounds like: taking care of yourself. Here are a few self-care practices I recommend for new dads:

1. **Meditation**: I know, I know - that sounds weird. But meditation has become increasingly popular due to its amazing effects on mental health and well-being. There are a lot of apps that teach simple meditation practices. One of my favorites is Healthy Minds, which combines simple meditations with short podcast-style lectures about the benefits of meditation. Taking just five minutes per day made a huge difference in my patience, anxiety levels, and stress levels.
2. **Exercise:** Exercise is a must for anyone who wants to practice self-care and improve their mood, not to mention their physical fitness. Take time at least once a week to play a sport you like or do a type of exercise you enjoy. The enjoyment factor is crucial here because you'll be much more likely to follow through if you choose a physical activity you look forward to.
3. **Sleep:** Getting enough sleep at night might seem like an impossible dream during your baby's first year, but if you're experiencing trouble in your relationship or mood challenges, it's critical you find a solution. Consider hiring a postpartum doula to help for a few weeks so you can get some good shut-eye, or schedule a daily rest time after work to help you unwind and relax. Avoid caffeine after 3 pm, and talk to your doctor if you start to experience symptoms of insomnia, like

premature waking, sleeplessness, extreme tiredness during the day, or problems with memory and focus.

Aside from self-care, the second aspect of nurturing your relationship is **reaching out for support.** As studies have revealed more about the prevalence of postpartum relationship challenges, couples' support groups have become increasingly popular. Support groups meet to discuss common challenges new parents face or to share experiences with postpartum mood disorders. It's easy to feel isolated and alone when you're having relationship struggles, so it can be a huge relief to talk to other parents who are in the same boat. To find couples' support groups in your area, talk to your doctor or counselor and ask for recommendations.

## FINANCES

Finances are a leading cause of strife in any relationship. When you factor in all the costs associated with having a baby, it's not surprising that money might cause a rift in your relationship.

In addition to discussing financial issues with your counselor, it's important to recognize that we all have different money personalities. Your partner might be your polar opposite when it comes to how she handles her money - but that doesn't have to mean imminent disaster. Like any other relationship issue, the key is to take the time to understand each other so you can work together and not be at odds.

Here are the seven most common money personalities, according to Ken Honda, author of the book *Happy Money* (which I highly recommend):

- Compulsive Saver: Saves money obsessively, is afraid of unnecessary spending
- Compulsive Spender: Spends money as an emotional response, feels remorse

- Compulsive Money-Maker: Prioritizes high income and craves recognition for wealth
- Indifferent-to-Money: Doesn't really care about money but is often in a good financial position
- Saver-Splurger: Combination of Saver and Spender
- Gambler: Combination of Spender and Moneymaker, takes large risks with money
- Worrier: Always worried about money and afraid of lack of freedom

Taking the time to identify which personality you and your partner have will go a long way in helping you achieve financial balance.

And of course, knowing what to expect in your child's first year of life also helps alleviate some of the stress you might feel about finances. For example, childcare can be very costly, so be sure to sit down several months before you start sending your baby to daycare and budget carefully for the costs.

## NEW DAD TIPS AND TRICKS

When our first child was born, I have to admit I was a little clueless about some of the challenges the first year would bring for my relationship with my partner. After an unexpected cesarean section, a challenging recovery, and a two-week stay in the hospital due to a severe breast infection that turned into abscesses, it's safe to say she and I were both a little stressed.

Now, six kids later, I can look back and see there were things I could have done differently that would have helped minimize the stress. Do I feel guilty I didn't do them then? No. As they say, hindsight is 20/20. But I would be remiss if I didn't share some of the lessons I've learned throughout my years as a dad. So without further ado, to conclude this chapter I thought I would include my top 3 new dad tips and tricks to relationship success.

1. **Anticipate Her Needs.** Don't wait for your partner to ask you to do some dishes or pick up the baby when he's crying. Just do it. A lot of times, we new dads feel a little reticent to offer help. Why? A lot of reasons. You might doubt your ability, or maybe you think your partner would rather just do the task herself. In my experience, the best strategy is to ask yourself, "What would I *really* want to be done right now if I were in her shoes?" If the sink full of dishes is calling out to you, don't even ask if she wants you to wash them. I can guarantee she won't complain if you take action without checking in first.
2. **Prioritize Togetherness.** If you're experiencing relationship struggles, that's your priority. Work, chores, and social expectations can wait. Find something you enjoy doing together, and do it every day. That could be taking a walk around the block, playing a game, or watching your favorite show. Whatever it is, make it the priority of your day.
3. **Say "Thank You":** Your partner has gone through a lot this year, and the words "thank you" are always welcome. Practicing gratitude has been shown to have huge benefits for mental health, and it's a great way to improve your relationship, as well. Compliment your partner often and tell her she's doing a good job.

Finally, don't forget physical affection. If your partner is struggling with intercourse, as is common in the first year postpartum, this can be sensitive, but remember - simple things like eye contact, a hug, or just holding hands can be great ways to show your love and gratitude.

Relationship struggles are common in the first year, but that doesn't mean they are inevitable. Being attentive to your partner's needs, prioritizing quality time, and displaying gratitude and affection will all help you weather the storm and get through your first twelve months as a family of three.

I'm sure the first year as a new dad has had its ups and downs - after all, you've done a pretty amazing and challenging thing this year. You have welcomed a new human being into your life, helped your partner recover from pregnancy and childbirth, and learned a lot about your own limits and potential. And if you're like me, you've probably also learned that fatherhood isn't just something that happens overnight - it's a constant journey.

This year you've watched your son or daughter develop from a tiny, helpless infant into a headstrong, mobile toddler. Through it all, your presence has made a huge difference. Fathers who are involved in their baby's life from the beginning not only feel closer to their children in the early years, but also set them up for success later in life. So keep up the great work - the adventure is just getting started!

Please leave a review.

If this book has helped you in any way, please leave a review so that others will find the book as well. Thank you for reading.

Click To Leave Review

*Scan to leave a review.*

# RESOURCES

*Attachment Parenting International.* (n.d.).

https://www.attachmentparenting.org/

CDC (2022). *Immunization Schedules by Age.* AAP

https://www.cdc.gov/vaccines/schedules/downloads/child/0-18yrs-child-combined-schedule.pdf

Centers for Disease Control and Prevention. (n.d.) *Milestone Checklist.*

https://www.cdc.gov/ncbddd/actearly/pdf/FULL-LIST-CDC_LTSAE-Checklists2021_Eng_FNL2_508.pdf

Ernst, H. (2018) *Timeline of Postpartum Recovery.* Healthline.

https://www.healthline.com/health/postpartum-recovery-timeline

Griffin, R. (2021). *How Will My Premie Grow and Develop From Birth to Age 2?* WebMD.

https://www.webmd.com/parenting/baby/preemie-development-birth-age-2

# FREE BONUSES

**Free Bonus #1   Baby Financial Planning**

In this book, you will learn all about the financial considerations of having a baby.

**Free Bonus #2 10 Activities to Learn Parenting Skills**

In this book, you will get tips on how to build parenting skills even before the baby is born.

**Free Bonus #3  Authentic Connections**

In this book, you will learn new skills to help you nurture your connection with your partner and bring it to a whole new level.

# BIBLIOGRAPHY

AAP (2022). *How to Keep Your Sleeping Baby Safe: AAP Policy Explained.* HealthyChildren.org. https://www.healthychildren.org/English/ages-stages/baby/sleep/Pages/A-Parents-Guide-to-Safe-Sleep.aspx

Alabama Public Health (n.d.). *Stomach Capacity* https://www.alabamapublichealth.gov/perinatal/assets/StomachCapacity.pdf

*Apgar Score.* (2015). ACOG. https://www.acog.org/clinical/clinical-guidance/committee-opinion/articles/2015/10/the-apgar-score

*Attachment Parenting International.* (n.d.). https://www.attachmentparenting.org/

*Babies stir up clouds of bio-gunk when they crawl.* (n.d.). EurekAlert! https://www.eurekalert.org/news-releases/833043

*Baby's First Tooth: 7 Facts Parents Should Know.* (n.d.). HealthyChildren.org. https://www.healthychildren.org/English/ages-stages/baby/teething-tooth-care/Pages/Babys-First-Tooth-Facts-Parents-Should-Know.aspx

Bigelow, A. E. (2020). *Mother–Infant Skin-to-Skin Contact: Short- and Long-Term Effects for Mothers and Their Children Born Full-Term.* Frontiers. https://www.frontiersin.org/articles/10.3389/fpsyg.2020.01921/full

Brown, L. C. (2021, April 12). *Managing plugged ducts, mastitis when breastfeeding.* Mayo Clinic Health System. https://www.mayoclinichealthsystem.org/hometown-health/speaking-of-health/managing-plugged-ducts-mastitis-when-breastfeeding

Canadian Pediatric Society. (2012) *Preventing choking and suffocation in children.* Pediatrics and Child Health. https://academic.oup.com/pch/article/17/2/91/2638862

CDC (2022). *Immunization Schedules by Age.* AAP https://www.cdc.gov/vaccines/schedules/downloads/child/0-18yrs-child-combined-schedule.pdf

Cheng, C. (2018) *Supporting Fathering Through Infant Massage.* The Journal of Perinatal Education. https://connect.springerpub.com/content/sgrjpe/20/4/200.abstract

DeGroot, DW. (2021) *The effect of pregnancy and the duration of postpartum convalescence on the physical fitness of healthy women.* PLos One. https://www.ncbi.nlm.nih.gov/pmc/articles/PMC8318247/

# BIBLIOGRAPHY

Dewar, G. (2022, March 11). *The authoritative parenting style: An evidence-based guide.* PARENTING SCIENCE. https://parentingscience.com/authoritative-parenting-style/

*The Effect of Kangaroo Care on Breastfeeding and Development in Preterm Neonates.* (2021). Journal of Pediatric Nursing. https://www.sciencedirect.com/science/article/abs/pii/S0882596321000609#:~:text=Kangaroo%20care%20stabilizes%20the%20neonate's,and%20increases%20breast%20milk%20intake.

Erlandsonn, K. (2007) *Skin-to-skin care with the father after cesarean birth...Birth.* https://pubmed.ncbi.nlm.nih.gov/17542814/

*Explore how to tell if your baby is hungry.* (2019, August 13). Comotomo. http://www.comotomo.com/hungry-baby-feeding-cues-and-stomach-size/

Faure, M., & Richardson, A. (2012). *Baby Sense: Understanding your baby's sensory world - the key to a contented child* (1st ed.). Metz Press.

Fisher, D. (2018) *Fathers in neonatal units: Improving infant health by supporting the baby-father bond.* Journal of Neonatal Nursing. https://www.sciencedirect.com/science/article/abs/pii/S1355184118300930

Food Allergy Nottingham (n.d.) *Are you sure it's lactose intolerance and not delayed cow's milk allergy?* https://www.foodallergynottingham.co.uk/news/are-you-sure-its-lactose-intolerance-and-not-delayed-cows-milk-allergy

Garthus-Niegel, S. (2018). *The Impact of Postpartum Posttraumatic Stress and Depression Symptoms on Couples' Relationship Satisfaction: A Population-Based Prospective Study.* Frontiers. https://www.frontiersin.org/articles/10.3389/fpsyg.2018.01728/full

Goodman, J. (2003) *Paternal postpartum depression, its relationship to maternal postpartum depression, and implications for family health.* Journal of Advanced Nursing: https://onlinelibrary.wiley.com/doi/abs/10.1046/j.1365-2648.2003.02857.x

*"Green" parenting tips.* (n.d.). UNICEF. https://www.unicef.org/armenia/en/stories/green-parenting-tips

Harrington, C. T. (2022, June 1). *Butyrylcholinesterase is a potential biomarker for Sudden Infant Death Syndrome.* eBioMedicine. https://www.thelancet.com/journals/ebiom/article/PIIS2352-3964(22)00222-5/fulltext

Hewitt, L. (2020) *Tummy Time and Infant Health Outcomes: A Systematic Review.* Pediatrics. https://publications.aap.org/pediatrics/article/145/6/e20192168/76940/Tummy-Time-and-Infant-Health-Outcomes-A-Systematic?autologincheck=redirected?nfToken=00000000-0000-0000-0000-000000000000

Hock, E. and Schirtzinger, M. (1992). *Maternal Separation Anxiety*. Society for Research in Child Development. https://srcd.onlinelibrary.wiley.com/doi/abs/10.1111/j.1467-8624.1992.tb03598.x

Honda, K. (2022, October 7). *There are 7 money personality types, says psychology expert. Which one are you?* CNBC. https://www.cnbc.com/2021/04/28/7-money-personality-types-and-the-pitfalls-of-each.html

Hui-Chin, H. (2004) *Antecedents and consequences of separation anxiety in first-time mothers.* Infant Behavior and Development. https://www.sciencedirect.com/science/article/abs/pii/S0163638304000141

Iftikhar, N., MD. (2020, June 30). *Dunstan Baby Language*. Healthline. https://www.healthline.com/health/baby/dunstan-baby-language

*Information and Treatment for Postpartum Pelvic Floor Issues.* (n.d.). Lifespan. https://www.lifespan.org/centers-services/pelvic-floor-disorders/conditions-we-treat/information-and-treatment-postpartum

Journal of Pediatrics (2014) *Infant Deaths and Injuries Associated With Wearable Blankets, Swaddle Wraps, and Swaddling* - NIH. (2014). https://pubmed.ncbi.nlm.nih.gov/24507866/

Karp, H. (2020) *The Happiest Baby Book – Fully Revised*. Happiest Baby. https://www.happiestbaby.com/products/the-happiest-baby-book-paperback

WIC (n.d.). *Low Milk Supply.* WIC Breastfeeding Support. https://wicbreastfeeding.fns.usda.gov/low-milk-supply

MacDonald, J. (2020) *How are you sleeping?* Journal of Affective Disorders. https://www.sciencedirect.com/science/article/abs/pii/S0165032720330111

Masters, M. (2022, August 23). *When Baby Growth Spurts Happen and the Signs to Look For.* What to Expect. https://www.whattoexpect.com/first-year/ask-heidi/baby-growth-spurts.aspx

Miller, P. (2014) *The benefits of attachment parenting for infants and children.* APA PsycNet. https://psycnet.apa.org/fulltext/2014-55579-001.html

Miller, R. *What Is the Experience of Babywearing a NICU Graduate?* Nursing for Women's Health. https://www.sciencedirect.com/science/article/abs/pii/S1751485120300726

NCBI. (2020). *Associations Between Mother-Infant Bed-Sharing Practices and Infant Affect and Behavior during the Still-Face Paradigm.* NIH. https://www.ncbi.nlm.nih.gov/pmc/articles/PMC7704549/

NCT. (2022, July 27). *Bleeding after birth: 10 things you need to know NCT.* NCT (National Childbirth Trust). https://www.nct.org.uk/life-parent/your-body-after-birth/bleeding-after-birth-10-things-you-need-know

Neuman, A. (2022, September 28). *How to Teach Baby 25 Key Words in Baby Sign Language.* https://www.thebump.com/a/how-to-teach-baby-sign-language

NHS website. (2021, November 18). *What should I do if I think my baby is allergic or intolerant to cows' milk?* nhs.uk. https://www.nhs.uk/common-health-questions/childrens-health/what-should-i-do-if-i-think-my-baby-is-allergic-or-intolerant-to-cows-milk/

Pecora, G. (2022, May). *Infant sleep and development.* Infant Behavior and Development. https://www.sciencedirect.com/science/article/abs/pii/S0163638322000339

Perkin, M. R., PhD. (2018, August 6). *Association of Early Introduction of Solids With Infant Sleep: A Secondary Analysis of a Randomized Clinical.* https://jamanetwork.com/journals/jamapediatrics/article-abstract/2686726

*Premies: Breastfeeding.* (2020, August 6). La Leche League International. https://www.llli.org/breastfeeding-info/premies-breastfeeding/

Quillin, S. (2004). *Interaction Between Feeding Method and Co-Sleeping on Maternal-Newborn Sleep.* Journal of Obstetric, Gynecologic, and Neonatal Nursing. https://pubmed.ncbi.nlm.nih.gov/15495703/

Ri-Hua, X (2009) *Prenatal Social Support, Postnatal Social Support, and Postpartum Depression.* Annals of Epidemiology. https://www.sciencedirect.com/science/article/abs/pii/S1047279709000799

Scarff, J. (2019) *Postpartum Depression in Men.* Innovations in Clinical Neuroscience. https://www.ncbi.nlm.nih.gov/pmc/articles/PMC6659987/

Sears, R (2022). *The Family Bed.* Parenting. https://www.parenting.com/baby/sleep/the-family-bed/

Scaccia, A. (2018, December 21). *Your Guide to Baby Massage.* Healthline. https://www.healthline.com/health/parenting/baby-massage

Skenazy, L. (2021). *Free-Range Kids: How Parents and Teachers Can Let Go and Let Grow.* Wiley.

*Sleep Safety.* (2022, November 14). Riley Children's Health. https://www.rileychildrens.org/health-info/sleep-safety

Unicef UK. (2022, February 13). *Co-sleeping guide for health professionals.* The Baby Friendly Initiative. https://www.unicef.org.uk/babyfriendly/baby-friendly-resources/sleep-and-night-time-resources/co-sleeping-and-sids/

Weisleder, A. and Fernald, A. (2013) *Talking to Children Matters: Early Language Experience Strengthens Processing and Builds Vocabulary*. Association for Psychological Science. https://journals.sagepub.com/doi/abs/10.1177/0956797613488145

Wen-Wang, R. (2020) *Prevalence of Prenatal and postpartum depression in fathers*. Journal of Affective Disorders. https://www.sciencedirect.com/science/article/abs/pii/S016503271931496X?via%3Dihub

*Where We Stand: Vitamin D & Iron Supplements for Babies.* (2022). HealthyChildren.org. https://www.healthychildren.org/English/ages-stages/baby/feeding-nutrition/Pages/Vitamin-Iron-Supplements.aspx

Zhao, T. and Kuhl, P (2016) *Musical intervention enhances infants' neural processing of temporal structure in music and speech*. PNAS. https://www.pnas.org/doi/pdf/10.1073/pnas.1603984113

# ABOUT THE AUTHOR

New Dad Support consists of dads and parenting professionals and experts whose passion is sharing their experience and expertise with new dads and dads-to-be.

Made in the USA
Columbia, SC
09 November 2024